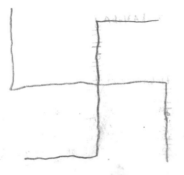

# ADOLF
# HITLER

# JOSHUA RUBENSTEIN

# ADOLF HITLER

FRANKLIN WATTS
NEW YORK | LONDON | TORONTO | SYDNEY | 1982
AN IMPACT BIOGRAPHY

A GROLIER COMPANY

Photographs courtesy of
United Press International Photo: pp. 18, 76;
National Archives: pp. 39, 46, 52, 57, 83, 112;
Culver Pictures: 63, 100

Library of Congress Cataloging in Publication Data
Rubenstein, Joshua.
Adolf Hitler.

(An Impact biography)
Bibliography: p.
Includes index.
Summary: A biography examining both the private and
public life of the struggling Austrian artist who rose
from obscurity to power as the head of the Nazi Party
and, eventually, the German nation.
1. Hitler, Adolf, 1889-1945—Juvenile literature.
2. Heads of state-Germany—Biography—
Juvenile literature. [1. Hitler, Adolf, 1889-1945.
2. Heads of state. 3. Germany—Politics and
government, 1933-1945] I. Title.
DD247.H5R78 1982 943.086′092′4 [B] [92] 82-11181
ISBN 0-531-04477-7

*acc. 6070*

# CONTENTS

ADOLF
HITLER

# INTRODUCTION

On April 30, 1945, Adolf Hitler committed suicide in an underground bunker near the center of Berlin. His dream of a "Thousand-Year Reich" lay in ruins. German cities had been bombed, German armies captured or destroyed. A week after Hitler's death, on May 8, Germany offered unconditional surrender to the Allied forces. The nightmare of World War II in Europe came to an end.

Adolf Hitler was not the only man responsible for the horrors of World War II. But it was his dream of world domination that possessed Germany. For twelve years he had the opportunity to make the world over in the image of his sick fantasies. He nearly succeeded.

Hitler was one of the most hated men in world history. But he cannot be dismissed as simply a monster who through the accidents of history reached great power. Hitler was a man whose prejudices and fears were shared by many other people. He gained their trust, even their adoration. Millions, after all, died fighting in his name. We must take Hitler seriously both as an individual and as an effective politician in order to understand how he gained so much power and how he abused that power. Only then will we be able to appreciate the profound evil of Hitler and Nazism.

# SEEDS OF
# HATE

# 1

Adolf Hitler was born on April 20, 1889, in the small Austrian city of Braunau near the German border. His father, Alois Hitler, worked as a customs official, checking goods that were traded between Austria and Germany. His mother, Klara, had worked for Alois Hitler as a maid before their marriage in 1885. Alois had been married twice before, but both his wives had died of tuberculosis. From these earlier marriages, he had two children, a boy called Alois after himself and a girl named Angela.

Klara treated these children with patience and love. She also gave birth to three children of her own who died in infancy. Adolf Hitler was his parents' fourth child. When he appeared to be sickly, his mother feared that he, too, would die. But Adolf grew stronger and lived.

Klara Hitler raised Adolf while his father worked long hours at the customs station. When Alois Hitler had free time he preferred to spend it with his friends or with his favorite hobby—beekeeping. Adolf Hitler, in his typically exaggerated style, once described the beekeeping activity of the Hitler family: "To be stung by a bee in our family was an ordinary, everyday occurrence. My mother often pulled out as many as forty-five or fifty stings from the old gentleman when he returned from cleaning hives. He never protected himself in any way; all he did was to smoke all the time—in other words, a good excuse for another cigar."

Alois Hitler was a respected customs official. He received a promotion in 1892 to the position of Higher Collector, giving him more responsibility for assessing customs duties on goods imported into Austria. After Austria and Germany signed a new tariff agreement the same year, the amount of trade between the two countries increased. Alois was transferred to Passau, a larger and more important city on the German side of the border. But he did not stay there long. After eighteen months the government transferred him again, this time to Linz, a city in Austria fifty miles east of Passau.

Klara and the children did not join him in Linz. A week before her husband's transfer Klara gave birth to another son, Edmond. Because she was afraid to travel with the baby, she stayed in Passau with her two sons and her stepchildren, Alois and Angela. Edmond's birth and then his father's leaving for Linz created a great change in Adolf's life. Until Edmond was born, a month before Adolf's fifth birthday, his mother had doted on him unceasingly. She had already lost three children, so Adolf, who overcame his initially weak appearance, became "the apple of her eye." Then suddenly in 1894 Adolf gained a good deal of freedom from his parents' supervision because his father moved to Linz and his mother now had to care for a new-born son. The older children were teenagers and were expected to help their stepmother around the house. Adolf had time to do as he pleased. For nearly a year he spent hours playing with the German children or wandering about by himself. He learned a Bavarian dialect of German, a form of speech that he used years later to hold the attention of millions.

The family remained separated for almost a year, until

April 1895, when Alois was about to retire after forty years of service. He was fifty-eight years old and could have worked for several more years, but he retired prematurely because of ill health. He bought a modest, nine-acre farm in the small town of Hafeld, where his wife and children joined him.

Alois had always dreamed of retiring peacefully to a farm where he could tend his bees and grow vegetables in a garden. But the farm proved to be harder to maintain than he had expected. Alois had not worked on a farm for over thirty years. He was nearly sixty years old, and his strength was limited. It was too much for him to keep nine acres of land profitably under cultivation.

Family life also disappointed him. Klara gave birth to a daughter, Paula, in January 1896, and Alois found his five children were noisy and troublesome. He had never liked to be around them, but now, retired on his farm, in a small, quiet village, he could not get away from them. His work on the farm was difficult and this probably made it harder for him to be patient with the children. His relationship with his oldest son, Alois, was especially troubling. The father demanded total obedience and was willing to beat his son, sometimes with a small whip, when he did not receive it.

Young Alois grew so resentful that in 1896, at the age of fourteen, he left home never to return. Alois became an unhappy adult. He was jailed twice for theft. He worked as a waiter in Paris, then moved to Ireland where he started a family. He never got along with his younger brother Adolf. Although she was kind to her stepchildren, Klara gave most of her attention to her own sons. But at the same time, Alois did not receive his father's love or understanding. As a result, he was jealous of Adolf. Years later, though, when Adolf became a famous political figure in Germany, Alois moved to Berlin and opened a cafe, hoping to take advantage of his family connection. Adolf did not like him, however, and would tell companions not to mention his brother's name.

Adolf liked his sisters more. He was close to his half-sister Angela, while his younger sister Paula was his favorite all his life. When he was the leader of Germany, Paula took charge of his household and remained loyal to him.

For several years Alois Hitler continued to move his family from one place to another. The burdensome farm was sold in 1897 and the Hitler family moved to Lambach, a small town of seventeen hundred inhabitants. The next year they all moved to Leonding near Linz. By the age of nine, Adolf had entered his third elementary school.

Tragedy, too, interrupted their lives when Adolf's younger brother Edmond died of measles on February 2, 1900. Adolf became the last son to remain at home. Alois Hitler had always wanted his sons to succeed, to excel at school and prepare for solid careers. But with three sons dead and young Alois run away from home, he now looked to Adolf for great things.


## SCHOOL DAYS

Adolf was a good student in elementary school. Energetic and smart, he was a leader among the children his age. He especially enjoyed warlike games. He would organize his classmates into "battles," choosing himself to be the captain. He also read a great deal, picking the stories of James Fenimore Cooper to inspire his games of soldiers and Indians. Adolf also had an outstanding gift as a speaker, even as a child. In his memoir *Mein Kampf*, which he wrote more than two decades later, he remembered: "I believe that even my oratorical talent was being developed in the form of more or less violent arguments with my schoolmates. I had become a little ringleader."

Adolf also discovered that he could draw. When other pupils were studying, Adolf would often sketch pictures from memory, dazzling his friends with castles and landscapes.

When he finished elementary school, Adolf and his parents had to decide about his future plans. Much depended on the secondary school Adolf would attend. He was eligible to choose either a *Gymnasium* or a *Realschule*. The *Gymnasium* focused on classical education, providing a solid background for university study. The *Realschule* had a more technical and scientific curriculum. Adolf's secret dream was to become an artist. But his father wanted him to become a civil servant, and decided that Adolf should attend the *Realschule*. Adolf agreed, mainly because the school had a course in drawing.

Adolf had to walk three miles to the *Realschule* in Linz. It was a large school, much bigger than his elementary school in the countryside. Adolf felt out of place here and did poorly in his work. The teachers could not give him the special attention he was used to and the other students looked down on children from the small, suburban villages. Adolf did better his second year and he became more popular among his classmates, leading them in games of cowboys and Indians.

Although Austria is a German-speaking country, its politics have historically been separate from Germany. Nevertheless, the two neighboring countries have shared similar social and cultural traditions, and when Hitler was a boy some Austrians felt a special attraction to Germany. Adolf, like many of his classmates at the *Realschule*, expressed a strong German nationalism and admiration for Prince Otto von Bismarck, the first Chancellor of the German Empire, who had died in 1898. He was also fascinated by the heroic figures of German mythology, an attraction that drew him to the operas of Richard Wagner, many of which are based on German myths. At the age of twelve he attended his first opera by Wagner at the Linz Opera House. From then on Adolf admired Wagner above all other composers.

Adolf's romantic dream of becoming an artist, his rebellious nature, and his admiration for Germany reinforced his conflict with his father who was an energetic supporter of the Austrian monarch and who wanted his son to choose the more conventional and secure life of a civil servant. Adolf and his father did not get along, and like his older brother, he was sometimes beaten for disobedience. Their troubled relationship, however, came to an end on January 3, 1903, when Alois Hitler collapsed and died at the age of sixty-five.

## THE ARTIST'S DREAM

Although Adolf no longer had to struggle directly against his father's wishes for him, his work in school did not improve, and he spent more time by himself, reading and drawing. His poor work in school caught up with him in 1905. Because of his failing grades he could not enter a high school. At the age of sixteen, without serious plans for working or studying, Adolf Hitler began spending most of his time at home.

Living in Linz, Hitler made his first adult friendship with a young musician named August Kubizek. They met at the Linz Opera House. The two teenagers found it easy to share their dreams of artistic achievement, Hitler as a painter and Kubizek as a musician. They went to the opera together and walked the streets of Linz. Hitler was becoming especially interested in architecture, a field that had intrigued him even as a small boy when he had enjoyed drawing castles and other buildings.

Klara and her children were not left penniless by Alois's death. He had worked for many years as a customs official and under Austrian law his widow and children received a generous pension after his death. In May 1906, Klara Hitler was able to give her son Adolf money to visit Vienna. He had dreamed of going to Austria's capital to see its museums and imperial grandeur. He stayed for a month, spending most of his time studying the city's monumental buildings. Hitler never lost his interest in architecture and architectural sketching.

Years after, when he became the most powerful leader in Europe, he would still devote time to devising models for new buildings and cities.

Adolf Hitler had a particularly close and loving relationship with his mother. She had spoiled him as an infant and later, when her husband died, Adolf became the center of the household, even though he was still a teenager and neither worked nor studied. She did not insist that he return to school or that he find work to help support the family. Adolf, in turn, was devoted to his mother. He sent her postcards when he traveled to Vienna and shared his dream of artistic success with her.

While Adolf was making little progress toward his goal of becoming an artist, his life grew much sadder by the fatal illness of his mother. In January 1907 the doctors found a malignant tumor in her chest. They operated immediately but as the year progressed she grew continually weaker. Hitler often met with her doctor, Edmund Bloch, and tried to comfort his mother as best he could.

At the same time, Hitler was eager to study art seriously. His trip to Vienna had inspired him and he wanted to return to the capital in order to enter the Academy of Fine Arts. In the summer of 1907 his mother gave her permission for Adolf to leave Linz. He was allowed to take his inheritance from his father (about 700 kronen or 170 American dollars today), enough to support him in Vienna for a year and to pay his tuition at the Academy.

Klara Hitler cried when her son left by train that September. She was worried about him, worried about his future. Her health was growing worse as well. But Adolf had to reach Vienna early in the fall because examinations for the Academy took place in October and he wanted to be prepared.

When October came, however, Adolf's application to the Academy was not accepted. The rector told him he had more promise as an architect than a painter. Hitler had barely recovered from his disappointment when he received an urgent letter from Linz: his mother was dying.

Hitler rushed back home. He stayed by her side, cooking meals and keeping the house in order with his sister Paula. As the weather grew colder his mother was moved to the kitchen, the only room that was heated all day. Adolf slept in the same room in case she needed him. But all his care could not save her. Klara Hitler died on December 21, 1907. Adolf was terribly shaken. "In all my career," Dr. Bloch later remembered, "I never saw anyone so prostrate with grief as Adolf Hitler."


VIENNA

The six years following his mother's death were the most difficult of Hitler's young adulthood. Determined to be an artist, he returned to Vienna in February still hoping to gain admission to the Academy of Fine Arts. But the school turned him down once again. Adolf grew increasingly bitter. He did not look for regular work but supported himself from what was left of his inheritance as well as from part of his father's pension. His friend August Kubizek joined him in Vienna where they shared a room; they would often go to the opera where Adolf never tired of hearing the works of Richard Wagner.

Vienna, at this time, was one of the great capitals of Europe, the center of the Austro-Hungarian Empire. Its imperial buildings, handsome parks, and energetic cultural life attracted people from all over the continent. Newspapers appeared in many different languages and the German flavor of the city seemed overwhelmed by the influx of Italians, Hungarians, Poles, and Slavs.

Like major cities everywhere, Vienna was a city of contrasts. But in the first decades of this century its contrasts were dangerously extreme. It was a city of fabulous wealth and degrading poverty, of time-worn custom and radical intellectual experiments, of diverse ethnic groups and angry racial hatred. There were strong currents of German nationalism and fanatical expressions of anti-semitism. Theodore Herzl, the founder of modern Zionism, worked as a journalist in Vienna. Sigmund Freud practiced medicine there and worked out his theories of human psychology. New developments in music, art, and philosophy also originated in Vienna.

Adolf Hitler came to Vienna full of hope for his career as an artist. But within a year his hopes were disappointed. After failing to pass the Academy's entrance examination in 1907 Adolf spent a year working hard to improve his artistic ability. He took painting lessons and produced new pictures to show the Academy. His talent as an architect became even more obvious. The Academy, however, refused him once again. Without regular work and his prospects for study dashed as well, he decided to break his ties to people who had been close to him. His friend Kubizek was out of town and when he returned to their apartment Kubizek learned that Adolf had moved away, leaving behind no new address. Kubizek was succeeding as a musician while Hitler seemed to be going nowhere. Rather than face his friend, Adolf had moved away.

He lived alone in cheap apartments or sometimes among other poverty-stricken, homeless men in special dormitories. They befriended him, showed him where to stay warm during the day, how to find food, how to beg for change on the Vienna streets. "Even now I shudder," he later wrote, "when I think of those pitiful dens, the shelters and lodging houses, those sinister pictures of dirt and repugnant filth."

Hitler lived like this for a year until one of his companions, Reinhold Hanisch, noted his talent for drawing and suggested that he produce postcards they could sell in taverns and on the street. Hitler responded to Hanisch's encouragement. The postcards sold well. Then Hanisch suggested that Adolf produce watercolor pictures—larger than the size of postcards—which could be sold for more money. Hitler could complete about one a day.

While Hitler continued his work as an artist, he spent a lot of time reading. He was especially interested in politics. But while he attended sessions of the Austrian parliament, his own political beliefs grew increasingly extreme, full of distrust of democracy, liberals, and trade unions, as well as Jews, Czechs, Poles, Hungarians, and other nationalities in the Hapsburg empire.

Vienna at this time was home to people of violent racial prejudice, and even the mayor, Karl Lueger, was an ardent anti-Semite. Journals and newspapers ranted against Jews and other Europeans who were said to be corrupting the Aryan—that is, the German—blood of the city. Hitler, like many others in the lower class, was attracted to these racial theories, and he became a dedicated anti-Semite, reading magazines and books that expressed nothing but hatred for Jews.

Adolf Hitler's turn to anti-Semitism occurred while his personality as a whole was changing. His mother's death was a painful experience for him. Then his failure to enter the Academy made him bitter. He could not accept responsibility for this; he could not recognize his own shortcomings as a painter. Instead, he blamed others. And he came to hate Vienna where his childhood dream of artistic success was shattered.

We cannot say for sure what caused Hitler to focus his hatred on the Jews and all liberal politicians. He knew many Jews. His mother's doctor had been a Jew, and Hitler always expressed gratitude for how Dr. Bloch tried to help her. He sold paintings in Vienna to Jewish art dealers. Nonetheless, Hitler came to hate Jews violently. It is important to remember that this occurred while his life was difficult and he was overcome by personal disappointment. He read a great deal, looking for the answers to his own unhappiness. When Hitler left Vienna in 1913 he not only hated Jews, but also despised his country, trade unions, democratic rule, and mankind in general. He respected only art and brutal power. By 1913, after more than five years in Vienna, what he later called "the most miserable time of my life," Hitler decided to move to Germany.

MUNICH

Adolf Hitler arrived in Munich by train in May 1913. He immediately fell in love with the city. He rented a room above a tailor shop near the student district which is still called Schwabing. Hitler had not given up his dream of becoming an artist. In spite of his experiences in Vienna he came to Munich intending to study art and architecture for three more years. Although he worked hard, producing pictures from his first days in the city, the commercial art market was not very strong and he was forced to sell his pictures in beer halls. But Hitler was not discouraged. He enjoyed life in Munich much more than in Vienna. He had time to study in the library and to argue with students and other writers and political activists in the city's bars and restaurants. Hitler was fascinated by politics. He was especially interested in Marxism and, as he recalled in *Mein Kampf*, it was in Munich that "I turned my attention to the attempts to master this world plague."

Marxism is a system of political and economic ideas that is based on the writings of the philosopher Karl Marx. Marx grew up in Germany but later spent many years in England where he devoted himself to studying history, politics, and economics. Living in England in the nineteenth century, Marx witnessed the industrial revolution when modern factories were first built and masses of workers streamed into the cities from the countryside. Marx saw the difficult living conditions these workers faced. He wanted to improve their status in society. Indeed, he advocated revolution as a means to overthrow capitalism in order to establish a socialist society which would be controlled by the workers.

Marx's ideas inspired revolutionaries throughout Europe and when Hitler was in Munich in 1913 many students, workers, and intellectuals shared Marx's dream of a communist society. Hitler did not. He spent long hours in the library formulating his own ideas and reinforcing his hatred of all liberal, socialist, and communist movements.

At the same time, he continued to struggle as an artist. Munich, at that time, was a center for artists in Europe. Many of them pursued artistic experiments, trying out different combinations of color and shape, moving away from purely representational art to more abstract images. Hitler did not move in this artistic direction. He had a genuine talent for drawing buildings and a fine sense of architecture. But it was not enough to earn a steady or reliable living.

WORLD WAR I

His struggling life as an artist came to an end in 1914. On June 28 Europe was shaken by the news that Archduke Franz Ferdinand, the heir to the Austrian throne, and his wife Sophie had been assassinated in Sarajevo by a young Serbian nationalist. The murder set off a seemingly uncontrollable series of events: Austria declared war on Serbia; Russia then mobilized her troops; then Germany responded by declaring war against Russia. Two days later the German Kaiser also declared war against France.

Hitler was thrilled by these events. He saw war as an adventure—a chance to defend his belief in German nationalism and to prove Germany's superior strength over England, France, and the detestable people of Poland and Russia. "Even today," he wrote ten years later in *Mein Kampf*, "I am not ashamed to say that, overcome with rapturous enthusiasm, I fell to my knees and thanked Heaven from an over-flowing heart for granting me the good fortune of being allowed to live at this time." Hitler volunteered for the German army and was accepted.

Just as no one thought that the assassination in Sarajevo would lead to war, so no one imagined when the war began that it would last very long. World War I—the Great War—lasted for four years and when it was over the map of Europe was never to be the same.

Hitler saw action on the western front facing British, French, and Belgian troops. He was a brave soldier, well-liked and admired by his comrades. World War I was not a war of quick offensive movement. On the western front especially, the soldiers of France and Germany dug themselves into long, deep trenches. They would live there for months at a time, enduring the cold of winter and the mud of springtime, while each side mounted small attacks across the no-man's land that divided the armies. During stretches of time in the trenches Hitler would amuse his friends with sketches and paintings. Working as a messenger, he was often subjected to heavy firing. He had to bring news and relay information and questions between units at the front, and from the front to superior officers behind the lines. He never refused danger-ous assignments, and several times he narrowly escaped death. Once an enemy artillery shell blew up regimental head-quarters just after Hitler had walked out. Another time, eating dinner in a trench with his friends, he had a premonition that he should get up and walk away, and he did so. The next minute a shell landed among his comrades, killing them all. For his bravery in the field, Hitler received six medals, includ-ing the Iron Cross, Germany's highest military honor.

After four years of war Germany had gained control of large areas on the eastern front, territory that is now part of Poland and the Soviet Union. But in the west, facing the

armies of France, England, and (after 1917) the United States, Germany faced imminent defeat. At home, the civilian population was tired of the war. Food supplies were dangerously low. Milk was unavailable, and bread was made from sawdust and potato peelings. Workers in Germany went on strike, demanding an end to the war, more food, and a democratic government in place of the Kaiser's monarchy.

Soldiers like Hitler reacted bitterly. What were they fighting for if the country did not want victory? Why should they suffer at the front if the people at home were not willing to make sacrifices as well?

In the midst of the war, in 1917, a revolution in Russia overthrew the monarchy of the Czar and declared a workers' state. Led by Vladimir Lenin and based on the principles of Karl Marx, this was the first successful socialist revolution. Germany and the new government of Russia, now called the Soviet Union, entered negotiations. They signed a treaty in the Russian city of Brest-Litovsk, bringing peace to the eastern front. Now the Kaiser and his generals hoped for a breakthrough in the fighting in the west. Massive attacks were launched into France. But they did not succeed. The morale of Germany's soldiers collapsed. They did not want to continue to fight.

Hitler was furious. He had fought valiantly in the trenches for four years but now he blamed socialists and pacifists back home for bringing Germany defeat. *They* wanted the war to end; *they* wanted Germany to admit defeat. Hitler hated them for stabbing Germany in the back.

*This photograph, which was used in a documentary film,* Hitler's Reign of Terror, *shows Hitler (left) in the uniform of a corporal in the German Army during World War I.*

On October 14, 1918, while Hitler's regiment was fighting near Ypres against the French, Hitler was blinded temporarily during an attack of mustard gas. He was removed from the front on a hospital train. The war came to an end in November while Hitler was recovering in Pasewalk, a city north of Berlin.

During his convalescence, just before the official end of World War I, insurrections broke out all over Germany. They were expressions of revolt against Kaiser Wilhelm II. Sailors organized a mutiny in Kiel, taking over most of the city. In Munich revolutionaries took over the government of Bavaria, proclaiming a republic of their own. Unable to command respect at home, and under pressure from the western allies, especially President Woodrow Wilson of the United States, Kaiser Wilhelm abdicated his throne. The German Empire came to an end and a new government led by social democratic politicians came to power.

It was the Kaiser and his generals who had directed, then lost the war. They were responsible for the enormous losses in the trenches of Verdun and in other battles where thousands and thousands of Germany's young men lost their lives to machine guns and artillery fire. But when the war ended, on November 11, 1918, the Kaiser and his generals were no longer in power. A representative of the new German government, a socialist, signed the armistice agreement with the western allies.

Adolf Hitler would never forgive any of them.

# PARTY, PRISON, POLITICS

# 2

On June 28, 1919, the victors of World War I concluded the Versailles Treaty in a palace on the outskirts of Paris. With little choice, the German government accepted its harsh terms. Germany had to accept responsibility for causing the war and pay for all civilian damage caused by the fighting. Germany was also required to give up territory: Alsace-Lorraine went to France, the Malmédy region to Belgium, a good chunk of Posen and West Prussia to Poland. Danzig, an area in northern Poland with a sizable German population, became a free state. The treaty also deprived Germany of its colonies in Africa.

To complete the humiliation, the Allies pledged to occupy the Rhineland for at least fifteen years and an area thirty miles wide on the right bank of the Rhine river was to be demilitarized. In addition, the German army was limited to one hundred thousand soldiers while the country was forbidden to have submarines or military aircraft.

The Versailles Treaty was meant to resolve the severe crisis in the European political system brought on by the war. Instead, the treaty made the crisis worse, for it came at a time when Germany itself was wracked by violence and attempted revolution.

## THE COMMUNIST THREAT

In Berlin a group of communist revolutionaries, calling themselves Spartacists after a famous Roman slave, took over the capital in January 1919. With the help of mutinous sailors, they gained control of the city's public transportation, its armaments factories, and public utilities. Workers in Berlin also supported the revolt. By January 6, two hundred thousand workers, carrying flags and weapons, marched through the streets of Berlin. Within a day, the revolutionaries held railroad stations and surrounded the chancellery where President Ebert was hiding. For a short time it looked as if Berlin and perhaps all of Germany would join the Soviet Union as a communist-dominated country. But within a week an army of right-wing soldiers, called the Free Corps, invaded Berlin and destroyed the attempted revolt.

In the aftermath of the war, there was a breakdown in the official military and police organizations and they could not handle the challenge posed by the revolutionaries. But many demobilized soldiers were disgusted with events back home. They feared a communist takeover and were willing to stop it. Military officials appealed to these men with billboard and newspaper announcements, asking them to rise up, to join the Free Corps, and crush the Spartacist revolt in Berlin. The Free Corps was an illegal army; it did not have official government sanction. But Germany was in such disorder that military officers could raise such an army on their own, outside the law, in order to resist the Spartacists. The fighting between the Free Corps and the Spartacists did not last long before the communists were defeated. Their leaders, Rosa Luxembourg and Karl Liebknecht, were hunted down and killed.

Within a few days the new republic that had been declared after the abdication of the Kaiser held its first national election. Women were allowed to vote for the first time in German history. Almost ninety percent of the eligible voters turned out, electing 423 deputies to the country's new parliament. Ebert's moderate socialists received forty percent of the vote, as did two politically centrist parties who also supported the republic. Two parties on the right who wanted a return of the monarchy received about fifteen percent of the parliamentary seats while a far-left socialist group received only seven percent.

Berlin was not considered safe enough to house the parliament so the deputies decided to meet in the small city of Weimar. For this reason the period between 1919 and 1933 is called the Weimar Republic. It was Germany's first attempt at political democracy and, tragically, it was a miserable failure.

Adolf Hitler was still in the army when the Weimar Republic was established. He had been discharged from the hospital in November 1918, having overcome the temporary blindness caused by the mustard gas attack. He reported to his regiment in Munich and from there went for duty to a prisoner-of-war camp in Traunstein, sixty miles east of Munich. He was not involved in the fighting between the revolutionaries and Free Corps units in Berlin or later in Munich. But he sympathized with the Free Corps, he shared their hatred of communism, and he was glad they crushed these revolts.

Inside the army, Hitler found new responsibilities. Under the terms of the Versailles treaty, the army, the *Reichswehr,* could not be larger than 100,000 men. Although it was a small army it still had influence within the country. The military authorities and the government of the Weimar Republic were determined to resist communist influence. So they recruited men to uncover subversive activity among the troops and to infiltrate workers' organizations. Hitler was asked to join this special unit. He was assigned to greet returning German soldiers, men who had themselves been captured during the fighting. They were bitter and hungry; many expressed solidarity with the revolutionaries. Hitler was part of a propaganda team that lectured these men on Germany's problems.

For years he had loved to argue over political and social issues, and his years at the front had sharpened his anger, making him an effective speaker. He gave the troops targets for their resentment, blaming "the Versailles disgrace" and "the Jewish-Marxist" conspiracy for Germany's troubles. His arguments took hold, and Hitler was thrilled by his new-found ability. "I started out with the greatest enthusiasm and love," he wrote in *Mein Kampf*. "For all at once I was offered an opportunity of speaking before a larger audience; and the thing that I had always presumed from pure feeling without knowing it was now corroborated; I could speak."

Hitler's superiors in the army appreciated his effectiveness. "Herr Hitler," one observer commented, "is the born people's speaker, and by his fanaticism and his crowd appeal he clearly compels the attention of his listeners and makes them think his way."

## THE GERMAN WORKERS' PARTY

In addition to his responsibilities as a lecturer, Hitler was asked to help investigate the many radical organizations that had emerged in Munich after the war. The whole range of political thinking was covered by these groups: superpatriots, communists, anarchists, racists, and violent German nationalists. Hitler was sent to attend a meeting of a tiny group called the German Workers' Party. He sat through the meeting but was not impressed. Only twenty-three people were in the room. The party's program was an unlikely combination of socialism, nationalism, and anti-Semitism. Ordered to attend a second meeting, Hitler reluctantly went back. This time perhaps forty people sat through the discussion. Hitler met the party's founder, Anton Drexler, a toolmaker in Munich's railroad yards. He impressed Hitler. Drexler's idea of "national socialism" combined Hitler's concerns as a fervent German patriot with his desire to improve the conditions of the working class. But Hitler did not want to join the German Workers' Party. It was a group of miserable men. He was looking for a way to get involved in Germany's political life and dreamed of forming his own political party, one he could mold and control on his own.

Hitler's superiors in the army, however, made up his mind for him. He had been reporting on the German Workers' Party to his commander, Captain Karl Mayr. Captain Mayr, in turn, shared these reports with his commanding officers, including General Erich Ludendorff. At the time, it was illegal for soldiers to join political parties, but Captain Mayr, under instructions from General Ludendorff, ordered Hitler to join the party and to help it grow. The army wanted to rebuild Germany's military power and recognized the need for workers' support. General Ludendorff saw the German Workers' Party as a place to begin attracting such support.

To appreciate Hitler's influence on history, it is important to understand how small and insignificant the German Workers' Party was when Hitler stumbled upon it: a handful of members with a few dozen more people attending its meetings. The members met off and on to complain about radicals in the streets, the Jews, and the lost war. Anton Drexler provided an outline of a program for the party. It would try to defuse the workers' attraction to Marxism by making the upper classes aware of their responsibility to the workers. The party was also cautiously anti-Semitic. But this meager program aside, the party had no concrete plans. It was more like a modest debating society.

Hitler set out to enlarge the party. He had invitations

mimeographed to encourage members to attend. When funds were available he placed advertisements in newspapers. Gradually the party attracted new members and the meetings grew in attendance. Hitler soon became the party's chief spokesman, giving speeches that helped raise money for the cause.

What stood out about Hitler was his manner of speaking. He did not address his audience in a calm, rational, or dignified manner. He would literally shout at them with threats and promises. His talks were very emotional and by their end he would have to slump into a chair exhausted, his face covered with sweat.

During this period, several people joined the party who would later play prominent roles in the Nazi movement. Hans Frank was a twenty-year-old law student when he first heard Hitler speak in a Munich beer hall. Two decades later Frank would take charge of German-occupied Poland. (Captured at the end of World War II, he would be tried and hanged at Nuremberg.)

Captain Ernst Rohm also became a member and a close friend of Hitler's. He brought many ex-soldiers into the party, changing the character of the German Workers' Party from a group of ineffectual, bitter men into a collection of tough and determined veterans. During meetings, especially when Hitler was speaking, people often started shouting, objecting to his violent language and his attacks on Jews. Rohm and his men, who were called "brownshirts" because of their uniforms, would intervene, beating up troublemakers and shoving them out of the hall. (Rohm and many of his soldier friends would be executed in 1934 on Hitler's orders. Once in power, Hitler no longer needed them.)

Another important and early colleague of Hitler's was Alfred Rosenberg. As editor of the party newspaper, Rosenberg published some of the worst racist propaganda. He introduced Hitler to the *Protocols of the Learned Elders of Zion,* a document that agents of the Russian Czar produced at the end of the nineteenth century. The *Protocols* outlined a Jewish plot for world domination. Hitler took the document seriously. It strengthened his hatred of Jews and his fear of Russian communism which he also believed was controlled by Jews. (Rosenberg remained an active leader of the Nazi party until the close of the war. Convicted of war crimes, he, too, was hanged at Nuremberg.)

## THE GROWTH OF THE NAZI PARTY

By the beginning of 1921, Hitler had turned the party into an important political force in Munich. As many as several thousand people would attend a rally sponsored by the party, with Adolf Hitler as the main attraction. The group also had a new name: the National Socialist German Workers' Party. (The word "Nazi" is a phonetic shortening of the German words for National Socialist.) It had a new symbol, too, the swastika. The word "swastika" is originally from the Sanskrit language; it means "all is all." The design had been used in Germany for centuries as a symbol for the sun or the cycle of life. Once Hitler adopted the swastika as his symbol, it took on a sinister, frightening quality that will never fade.

As Hitler's public role as a political figure became more prominent, it was important for him to leave the army. On March 31, 1920, he became a private citizen, but he still maintained close contact with military officers, particularly with General Ludendorff.

Hitler's genius as a politician was his sense of timing and his absolute confidence in his own ability to get his way, if only by the force of his personality. He was always looking for opportunities to give the party more publicity, even notoriety, anything to draw people to the cause. In January 1921 he organized the Nazis' first national congress. Only 411 members attended, but Hitler was not discouraged. Another opportunity quickly arose.

That winter had been cruel for the people of Germany.

Riots broke out over lack of food. The Allies, meeting in Paris, demanded large war reparations from the Germans as part of the Versailles agreement. All the major political parties wanted to protest, but they were afraid of organizing a demonstration in Munich. The communists, they feared, would attack them in the streets. But Hitler was not afraid. His storm-troopers, Rohm's SA, would protect him. The party hesitated though, so Hitler, who was tired of his colleagues' lack of resolve, rented a large hall himself. He also organized a lot of publicity on short notice, even sending two trucks bedecked with Nazi banners and loudspeakers into Munich streets. It was the first time a non-Marxist party had dared to use propaganda trucks in Munich.

His fellow Nazis were worried. They feared that only a handful of people would attend, making the party look foolish for renting a circus auditorium that held six thousand people. But Hitler's gamble paid off. Thousands attended the meeting, waiting in the cold and snow of a February night to get a seat. Hitler's approach was succeeding. He wanted to exploit every crisis, to make people believe the Nazis had an answer to Germany's problems. Hitler knew many Germans were looking for someone to blame, for an easy solution, for a way to express their frustration over Germany's helplessness, her defeat in the war, and the excessive demands of the victorious Allies. His speech that night was called "Future or Ruin." He demanded that Germany recognize its enemies within and outside the country. He ranted about Jews, about communists. Applause interrupted his remarks and the audience, roused to an emotional fervor, ended the meeting by singing a German nationalist song.

As Hitler's party grew in importance, he became widely known in Munich. Although he lived alone in a small, single room, he spent his evenings in the city's cafes, beer halls, and coffeehouses, talking with his friends and observing the life of the city. Wealthy families with conservative political leanings invited him to dinner and gave his party substantial financial support.

Most of his time, though, was spent in organizing the Nazi party. He and his fellow Nazis grew increasingly bold. Rohm's stormtroopers grew into a private army, not only designed to protect Hitler but also to break up meetings of Hitler's opponents. The Nazis took to the streets as well, starting fights and physically attacking Jews.

At the same time, the country's economy was growing weaker. Inflation took on absurd, almost comical dimensions. In 1918 one American dollar equaled 7.45 German marks. By 1923 the value of the mark had plummeted to 6,750 to the dollar! Two weeks after French and Belgian troops occupied the Ruhr in January 1923, because Germany had not paid its reparations, the mark fell even more drastically, to 50,000 against the dollar. By the end of the year, it took more than six million marks to equal a single prewar mark. The middle class lost its savings. German workers and their families could barely afford to buy food. A worker earning two billion marks a week could buy only potatoes for his family to eat.

In Bavaria especially there was much talk of revolution. Former soldiers were fed up with the Weimar Republic. They dreamed of making Bavaria independent of the rest of Germany, with Munich as the capital, or perhaps using Bavaria as a stepping-off point to take control of all of Germany. That was Hitler's plan. In November 1923 he tried to put it into effect.

## THE BEER HALL PUTSCH

Bavaria had always been more conservative, more nationalistic, than other parts of Germany. At a time when the Weimar Republic was governed by moderate democratic politicians, Bavaria was led by a group of former military commanders who did not like the Weimar Republic. Nevertheless, they were not prepared to take direct military action. Hitler decided to arrest them and take control of Bavaria himself. His attempt at revolution is remembered as the Beer Hall Putsch, "putsch" meaning rebellion in German.

On the night of November 8, 1923, Hitler and a large group of Nazis took over a meeting that had been organized by the three leaders of Bavaria: Gustav von Kahr, the state commissioner; General Otto von Lossow, the army commander; and Colonel Hans Seisser, head of the state police. Three thousand people were in the beer hall, listening to Bavaria's leaders. Hitler stood in the back of the room drinking a beer. Suddenly, while Kahr was speaking, Hitler forced his way to the platform followed by a phalanx of stormtroopers. Hitler's men blocked the exits and set up a machine gun to cover the audience. The crowd reacted with confusion and anger. Hitler, to gain their attention, fired his pistol into the ceiling. As the amazed crowd watched a revolution in front of their eyes, Hitler placed Kahr, Lossow, and Seisser under house arrest. Then he announced his intentions: "The task of the provisional German National Government is to organize the march on that sinful Babel, Berlin, and save the German people. . . . I am going to fulfill the vow I made to myself five years ago when I was a blind cripple in the military hospital: to know neither rest nor peace until the November criminals had been overthrown, until on the ruins of the wretched Germany of today there should arise once more a Germany of power and greatness, of freedom and splendor."

Hitler needed the cooperation of the three men he had arrested. They still commanded authority among the police and the army. Hitler promised to give them expanded powers once his revolution succeeded in seizing Berlin. The three men hesitated. Hitler threatened them with his pistol but they did not give in. Only when General Ludendorff arrived did the three men agree to support Hitler.

Meanwhile, in other parts of Munich, Nazi stormtroopers took up positions around key government buildings. Other Bavarian officials were arrested. Hitler's plan was proceeding successfully until he made two mistakes. While he was in the beer hall, he received word that his men were arguing with soldiers at the engineers' barracks. Hitler decided to leave his command post to resolve the matter. This was one mistake. The second was that he left General Ludendorff in charge of Kahr, Lossow, and Seisser.

As soon as Hitler left, General von Lossow announced that he needed to go to his office. General Ludendorff accepted his request and let him go. Soon after, Kahr and Seisser left as well. Hitler was furious when he returned. He knew they would oppose him once they were freed while Ludendorff was naive enough to think that because the three men had promised to support Hitler they would not go back on their word Ludendorff was mistaken.

From then on, Hitler's plan began to unravel. General von Lossow ordered troops from nearby cities to converge on Munich. By morning army and police units were in the streets of Munich to oppose Hitler's stormtroopers. Hitler thought he might still have a chance to succeed. He ordered his men to march into the heart of Munich, hoping to rally public opinion to his side.

His column of two thousand men moved off around noontime. Ludendorff, walking beside Hitler, was sure army men would not fire upon them. At one bridge, the Nazis broke through a small force of police without a shot being fired. But then the column reached Odeonsplatz, a major square in Munich. A cordon of state police blocked their way. A Nazi fired first, killing a sergeant. The police returned the fire, scattering the marchers off the streets. Hitler's bodyguard was killed as he stepped in front of his master. In all, eighteen men died in the shooting—fourteen followers of Hitler and four policemen. Hitler was injured when Ulrich Graf, his dying bodyguard, pulled him to the ground, painfully dislocating Hitler's left shoulder.

The Putsch was over.

Hitler managed to go into hiding for only a few days. His colleagues picked him up from the street and drove him out of Munich, wanting to get their wounded leader into Austria. But Hitler did not want to leave Germany. His arm was swollen, too, and terribly painful. He needed medical care and rest. While riding south, he remembered that some friends, the Haufstaengls, owned a small villa not far from Munich. At Hitler's suggestion, his party of men headed there.

The police found Hitler three days later. When he learned they were coming for him he expressed a desire to commit suicide, believing that his cause was lost. But his friend Helene Haufstaengl challenged him not to lose hope or courage. She took his revolver from his hand and hid it in a flour bin.

Hitler was taken to prison in Landsberg, a city forty miles west of Munich. The newspapers ridiculed his attempted coup, calling it "a beer hall revolution." The *New York Times* declared that Hitler and his followers were finished in politics. Dejected, in severe pain from the shoulder dislocation, Hitler sank into a deep depression. His attempt at revolution had turned into a joke. He thought no one would take him seriously in the future. He wanted to die. He ate hardly any food for two weeks until his followers, who were allowed to visit him, convinced Hitler that his death would only comfort his enemies. Gradually, he recovered his energy and determination, mainly because his many admirers showed their loyalty and belief in his ability.


TRIAL AND IMPRISONMENT

By February, when his trial began in Munich, Hitler was ready to defend himself. Although he was the one on trial, along with nine others, including General Ludendorff, Hitler never allowed the court to subdue him or break off his endless speeches. Foreign journalists found it hard to believe they were at a trial. Hitler, who was the principal defendant, did most of the accusing, blaming communists for threatening Germany. Once he spoke for four hours. The judge could not keep him quiet. Hitler denied nothing, taking full responsibility for the Putsch and explaining that he only wanted to lead Germany back to a position of strength and honor in the world. The prosecution charged that Hitler was seeking power to satisfy his own personal ambitions, that, for example, he wanted to head a government ministry. Hitler ridiculed these charges.

"I dreamed of becoming the destroyer of Marxism," he told the court. History had chosen him and it was absurd, he declared, to accuse him of petty ambitions. "The man who is born to be a dictator is not compelled—he wills; he is not driven forward—he drives himself forward. There is nothing immodest about this. . . . The man who feels called upon to govern a people has no right to say: If you want me or summon me, I will cooperate. No, it is his duty to step forward."

Despite his brave words, Hitler was found guilty of treason and armed revolt. The court, however, granted him a light sentence of five years in prison. Hitler could also have been deported to Austria as an undesirable alien, but the judges remembered his valor as a German soldier and refused to send him out of Germany. Hitler, instead, was returned to Landsberg prison.

Hitler's time in prison marked an important turning point in his life. He had been so involved in party affairs—running meetings, raising money, preparing speeches—that he had neglected to think about his broader goals or how he would resolve Germany's economic problems. Now, sitting in prison, he had plenty of time to read and think. Even before his trial he had developed the idea of constructing a system of broad highways that would make it easier to travel inside Germany. Then he would order engineers to design a small, economical car that would be mass-produced and made available to the German people. These plans would be put into effect later when Hitler ordered the construction of Germany's autobahns and the Volkswagen automobile.

Hitler also began writing a book. At first, he wanted to call it *Four and a Half Years of Struggle Against Lies, Stupidity, and Cowardice.* Later his publishers changed it to *Mein Kampf* or *My Struggle.* It is one of the most important and certainly one of the ugliest books of our century. Although few people took it seriously when it first appeared in 1925, Hitler sincerely and with great feeling described his intentions to restore Germany to a position of power and the longing to deal with the Jews. Fifteen years later, when German troops occupied almost all of Europe, no one had the right to utter surprise.

*Mein Kampf* begins like a sentimental schoolboy's diary, with Hitler recounting where he was born and his father's struggle to support a growing family. Gradually, though, the book turns into a rambling, at times incoherent description of Hitler's view of the world, the troubles caused by Jews, and what Hitler intends to do about it. There is no mistaking his racist attitudes, his hatred for Jews, or the blame he places on them for the crisis that beset Germany.

Hitler regarded race as the fundamental principle of human existence. "The racial question," he wrote in *Mein Kampf,* "gives the key not only to world history, but to all human culture," because, he believed, "in the blood alone resides the strength as well as the weakness of man." Hitler believed that the German people—"the Aryan race"—was the "bearer of human cultural development." Therefore, they were destined to rule the world. But the Jews, according to Hitler, threatened the fulfillment of this destiny. "The mightiest counterpoint to the Aryan is represented by the Jew." In Hitler's mind, the Aryans represented the perfection of human development, while the Jews were the embodiment of evil.

Faced with this threat, Hitler saw himself as a Messiah, a savior, who would protect and save Germany. "Therefore, I believe today," he proclaimed in *Mein Kampf,* "that I am acting out the will of the Almighty creator: By warding off the Jews I am fighting for the work of the Lord."

Another theme of *Mein Kampf* posed a direct threat to countries east of Germany. Hitler believed that Germany needed more *lebensraum* or living space, that her population needed more land to support its growth. He declared his intention to guarantee "the existence on this planet of the race embraced by the state, by establishing between the number and growth of the population on the one hand, and the size and value of the soil and territory on the other hand a viable, natural relationship. . . . We terminate the endless German drive to the south and west of Europe and direct our gaze towards the lands in the East. . . . If one wanted land and soil in Europe, then by and large this could only have been done at Russia's expense."

## DISCIPLINING THE NAZI PARTY

Hitler had been sentenced to five years in prison. If he had served out his term, the Nazi party might never have gained political dominance of Germany. His colleagues argued among themselves. Drexler attacked Hitler personally, calling him a dictator who had ruined the party with his attempt at revolution. After the failed Putsch, the Nazi party had been declared illegal, so Hitler's followers, together with General Ludendorff, formed a new party, the National Socialist Freedom Movement. In the national elections of May 1924 their slate received almost two million votes, electing thirty-two representatives to Germany's parliament, the Reichstag. General Ludendorff claimed credit for the modest triumph, but actually it was Hitler whose speeches in court attracted the attention of people to the radical combination of patriotism and racism. Outwardly, Hitler had to welcome the electoral success, but he was worried that the new party, led by General Ludendorff, would swallow up the Nazi movement and leave him without a political base.

Hitler, however, was not forced to serve his entire term. He was released less than a year after his trial, on December 20, 1924. Driven to Munich, he found his apartment filled with neighbors, flowers, and food to celebrate his return. But Hitler was anxious to get back to work. First, he needed to assess the current situation inside the country and within his own party. His colleagues were divided among themselves, and membership in the outlawed Nazi party had dwindled to about seven hundred. Germany, though, had grown stronger. The Allies, especially France, were now more conciliatory. A new, more reasonable schedule for paying war reparations had been worked out. With American investments helping Germany rebuild her economy, the mark was more stable and inflation much less of a problem.

Furthermore, after the disruptions of World War I, Germany was resuming her role as a leader of European culture. In spite of severe economic and political difficulties, Germany was still one of the most advanced societies in the world. Her universities were serious centers of learning. Her writers and poets were widely translated. Her composers and painters explored new areas of artistic expression. The Germans, in short, formed a vibrant, creative society. These qualities made it harder for the Nazis to gain power. Hitler would have to wait for a crisis.

Meanwhile, Hitler understood the changed mood of the country. He knew the time had passed for armed revolt, that now he would have to gain power more slowly, legally, through electoral politics. Within the Nazi party, however, arguments had erupted between those who supported armed

*This photograph of Hitler was taken on the day
he was released from Landsberg prison in 1924.*

revolution and those who urged a more conservative and gradual takeover. Hitler now had no intention of tolerating divisive arguments within the party. To achieve his aim he needed a unified party, one he could control absolutely.

Hitler also needed to regain the legal right to speak in public. Just after New Year's, Hitler called upon the Minister President of Bavaria, Heinrich Held. The two men spoke for half an hour, with Hitler offering his loyalty and willingness to help the government. This visit paid off five weeks later when the Bavarian government removed its restrictions on the National Socialist German Workers' Party. The party newspaper, the *Volkischer Beobachter*, could again appear and its leader, Adolf Hitler, was permitted to return to public life.

But Hitler moved too fast, almost wrecklessly. On February 27, he gave a speech in the same beer hall where his Putsch had begun. Four thousand people crowded the hall while another thousand tried to get in. Hitler was a hero. As an uprising, his Putsch had failed, but as a political gesture, it had been a great success. By going to prison Hitler had earned the respect of all the right-wing, nationalist parties. Everyone was willing to support him. To this receptive audience he appealed for unity and insisted that he be recognized as undisputed leader of the party. He also inflamed the audience with violent cries, urging them to "Fight Marxism and Judaism not according to middle-class standards but over corpses."

Words like these angered the authorities, and Hitler was again banned from speaking in Bavaria. The decree lasted for two years and spread throughout most of Germany. The government hoped to silence him but Hitler turned the ban to his own advantage, shifting his energy to gain complete and absolute control of the Nazi party. Since he could not speak in public, he spoke to small gatherings in the homes of his supporters. Hitler understood the importance of grass-roots organizing. He spent time meeting people throughout Munich, gaining their confidence and solidifying their support. It was during this period that his supporters began referring to him as the "Führer," the unquestioned leader of the party.

It was crucial for Hitler to strengthen the party's organization at this time because the Weimar Republic, under the leadership of Gustav Streseman, was achieving a degree of stability and economic prosperity. The popularity of the Nazis was fading. In the national elections of 1928, for example, the Nazis received less than three percent of the vote, sending only twelve deputies to the Reichstag. But the Nazis survived this crisis because Adolf Hitler imposed his own will and discipline on his colleagues.

Hitler dominated other men in the party who had ideas of their own. Ernst Rohm, for example, wanted his stormtroopers to have greater independence. But Hitler understood he could never come to power unless the German army supported him. He saw Rohm's SA, the stormtroopers, as the party's muscle rather than an independent revolutionary army which could challenge the German army. In addition, Hitler saw the need to put violent methods aside. So Rohm resigned and left for South America where he lived for five years before returning to help Hitler once again.

Another important figure was Gregor Strasser. He was the leader of a faction within the Nazi party that considered itself genuinely socialist. Strasser and his followers shared Hitler's extreme German nationalism. But they were also champions of the workers. They defended the rights of trade unions. They wanted state ownership of all land and were opposed to the power of corporations. Hitler did not share these principles. Strasser had gained prominence in the party while Hitler was in Landsberg prison. Like Hitler, he was an effective speaker and a talented political organizer. Hitler saw there were Nazis, particularly in northern Germany, where

Strasser worked, who hoped Strasser would one day lead the party. Hitler did not want to see the party divided over any issue of substance or over a challenge to his leadership.

To defeat Strasser, Hitler called a special meeting of the party leadership in Bamberg, a city far to the south where it was too inconvenient for many of Strasser's supporters to attend. Hitler did not want to alienate Strasser or his talented secretary Joseph Goebbels. So he did not attack their ideas. Instead, he made an eloquent plea for party unity which they could not oppose. By force of personality, Hitler dominated the conference, demanding that the party renounce democratic procedure and forbid splinter groups. Everyone had to pledge his allegiance to him alone. Otherwise, Hitler declared, he would resign. That settled the matter. Gregor Strasser remained Nazi party leader in northern Germany, but he was no longer a threat to Hitler's authority. From now on, whatever Hitler decided became the party's program.

PRIVATE LIFE

While Adolf Hitler gave himself completely to the Nazi cause, he also found time for more private moments. Until the day before he died he refused to get married, not wanting to compromise his commitment to politics. But he did have several important relationships with women.

Early in the 1920s, rich women in Munich were among Hitler's most significant financial backers, inviting him to their homes where he made contacts with other wealthy, conservative families. Hitler could be extremely charming in private conversation, kissing a woman's hand when he met her and being unfailingly polite and courteous when a woman was in a room with him. In reality, however, Hitler had a low opinion of women, believing them to be vain and prone to easy jealousy. Women were only interested in the attention of men, Hitler believed, and had no intellectual faculties of their own.

Despite these condescending views toward women, Hitler was still capable of deep and tender love. For several years he was close to his niece, Geli Raubal, the daughter of his sister, Angela. She was twenty years younger than her uncle. In 1929 Hitler moved out of his modest one-room apartment into a spacious nine-room apartment in a fashionable area of Munich. Geli studied singing off and on in the city, and when Hitler moved to his new apartment, she joined him there.

Although Hitler was devoted to Geli, he would not consider marriage. Hitler was not faithful to her either and by 1931 he was involved in a relationship with a second woman, Eva Braun. Hitler met her in a photo supply store where she worked. He liked to visit her there, bringing flowers and other gifts. They would go for walks, visit the Opera, or arrange picnics outside the city. But Geli still loved Hitler deeply; his flirting with Eva Braun drove Geli to despair. On September 18, 1931, she shot herself through the heart in Hitler's Munich apartment. Hitler was in Nuremberg when his deputy Rudolf Hess called him with the tragic news.

Geli Raubal was buried in Vienna. Hitler made a secret trip by car to the cemetery. He was not allowed to enter Vienna because of his politics—his extreme German nationalism meant trouble for his native Austria—but he chose to run the risk of arrest in order to leave flowers at her grave.

One curious result of Geli's suicide was Hitler's decision to become a vegetarian. He had toyed with the idea before, but a few days after his visit to Geli's grave site, Hitler refused to eat a piece of ham. "It is like eating a corpse," he told Hermann Göring. Hitler, apparently, never ate meat again, except for occasional servings of liver.

Geli's death sent Hitler into a deep depression. He may even have tried to shoot himself, but Eva Braun helped to revive his spirits. With her care, Hitler gradually regained his mental balance. He returned her love and by 1932 they were living together in his apartment. Eva Braun, however, also had good reason to be jealous. Hitler would not marry her either and he had many opportunities to pursue other women. In despair, Eva Braun tried to kill herself twice. In 1932 she attempted to shoot herself in the throat and in May 1935 she took an overdose of sleeping tablets. Both attempts failed. She stayed with him another ten years, through triumph and defeat, until April 1945 when Hitler, realizing the war was lost and his own capture imminent, agreed to marry her the night before they committed suicide.

POLITICIAN AND DEMAGOGUE

It is not, however, for these human qualities that most people remember Adolf Hitler. He is generally associated with violence and war and racism. The public image of Hitler is of a man making angry speeches to vast audiences who yearned to hear him denounce Jews and Marxists and proclaim Germany's racial and historical destiny. Hitler was a demagogue, what the dictionary defines as a "person who tries to stir up the people by appeals to emotions and prejudice in order to win them over quickly and so gain power." Germany faced severe economic and social problems in the 1920s, but Hitler's program was based more on finding scapegoats for these problems than on offering workable solutions. The Jews of Germany were not responsible for Germany's defeat or for the humiliating conditions imposed by the Versailles treaty. Yet Hitler was able to convince larger and larger sections of the German population, in particular from the lower classes, that the Jews were to blame for the country's economic difficulties. They became Hitler's scapegoats. If something could be done about the Jews, Hitler insisted, Germany would be a better and stronger country.

Although Hitler was a demagogue, he was no fool. Indeed, he was a masterful politician who knew when to be patient and when to strike. Hitler understood that his movement could not succeed without a severe crisis, one that would scare German voters and make them look for an extreme solution to their woes. From 1925 to 1929 Germany seemed to recover her stability, so the fortunes of the Nazi party waned. Hitler needed a national disaster in order to succeed. The death of the German Chancellor Gustav Streseman on October 3, 1929, and the deepening worldwide depression gave Hitler the occasion he was waiting for.

The German economy was heavily dependent on support from abroad, especially from the United States, and this help had enabled Chancellor Streseman and his government to improve the German economy. By 1929, however, unemployment was growing in Germany, leaving three million people out of work. Then in October the stock market crashed in New York, bringing on the Great Depression. With U.S. banks and corporations unable to support investments overseas, the German economy simply collapsed. Many countries, including the United States, endured similar difficulties: factories closed, jobs disappeared, banks failed. But Germany had only barely survived the terrible years following World War I. Her people did not have the spiritual or material resources to withstand another crisis. Faced with disaster (there were 6 million unemployed by 1932) more and more people turned to Adolf Hitler.

Hitler's appeal grew while he relied on a complicated game of parliamentary politics to gain power. Under the Weimar Republic, the people voted directly for a president who then asked a leading politician, usually the leader of a party that controlled a majority of seats in the Reichstag, to be Chancellor and to form a government. Under this type of parliamentary system, the President has limited political power while the Chancellor, or Prime Minister, chooses members of the cabinet and initiates legislation. Gustav Streseman had been a popular and effective Chancellor, but after his death

*Hitler is shown here with a group of Nazi supporters in 1931, when the party was enjoying great success in parliamentary elections.*

no political figure was able to put together a stable government. In the parliamentary election of March 1930 ten political parties each gained over a million votes, so new elections had to be called.

It was then that Hitler sensed his time had come. He campaigned furiously, crossing Germany by train, car, and airplane. He delivered twenty major speechs in the final six weeks of the campaign. Hitler concentrated on winning the masses. He had a message for each sector of the population. For the workers, he promised relief from unemployment. For the farmers, he offered higher prices on agricultural goods. For the students, he put forward an idealistic image of Germany, a moral crusade to revive German life. Again and again, he attacked Marxists and Jews. Dr. Goebbels used his brilliant methods of propaganda, blanketing Germany with red posters, organizing political rallies throughout the country.

The Nazis scored a great success. In 1928 they had won only twelve seats in the Reichstag. In September 1930 they polled more than six million votes and increased the size of their parliamentary delegation to one hundred seven.

Adolf Hitler wanted to become Chancellor of Germany, but it took him another two and a half years to reach his goal. He used the time well, campaigning for elections, making deals with leaders of other parties, building his private army, the SA, to fight communists in the streets of German cities. Meanwhile, Paul von Hindenburg, the aging President of Germany, tried to find an effective Chancellor. Hindenburg was a renowned general, probably the most beloved political figure in the country, but he was past eighty. His influence was growing weaker. He could not maintain confidence in the government by his own efforts, and no one appointed Chancellor seemed able to form a stable government. One politician after another failed. The Weimar Republic seemed doomed. Democratic parties in the center lost support while the Nazis on the right and the communists on the left grew in power.

After the elections of July 1932 Hitler controlled 238 seats in the Reichstag out of a total of 608. Hindenburg, however, did not want to appoint Hitler as Chancellor. He did not like Hitler and regarded his political rhetoric as too extreme. Nevertheless, by the start of 1933, Hindenburg had no choice. General Kurt von Schleicher, the incumbent Chancellor, could not maintain control of the Reichstag. He suggested that Hindenburg declare a state of emergency, dissolve the Reichstag, and give the Chancellor power to rule by decree. Hindenburg refused, and when the other parties learned of von Schleicher's plan, he was forced to resign.

With no one else to turn to, Hindenburg grudgingly asked Adolf Hitler to form a new government. On January 30, 1933, Hitler was appointed Chancellor of Germany. His dream was coming to fruition. All the years of organizing, of giving speeches in beer halls and auditoriums, were no longer in vain. Hitler now had the chance to make his fantastic dreams a reality.

# THE POWER OF THE THIRD REICH

## 3

Hitler's appointment as Chancellor of Germany on January 30, 1933, brought intense rejoicing among his followers. Crowds surged through the streets of Berlin, carrying banners and singing Nazi songs. Joseph Goebbels, who had become Hitler's propaganda chief, staged an impressive procession, with stormtroopers holding thousands of torches. Approaching Hitler's new office, the marchers shouted their triumphal cry, "Heil, Heil, Seig Heil!" Hans Frank, one of Hitler's longtime colleagues, stood near him that night. Years later, after his own conviction for war crimes, Frank stated: "God knows our hearts were pure that day and if anyone had told us of the events to come, no one would have believed it, least of all I. It was a day of glory and happiness."

Other experienced political figures, like Franz von Papen who became Vice-Chancellor, thought they could control Hitler. Aside from Hitler, only two other Nazis, Hermann Göring and Wilhelm Frick, were in the cabinet, Göring as President of the Reichstag, Frick serving as Interior Minister. This meant that Hitler would have to get along with members of other political parties in order to lead the government. These politi-

cians thought Hitler was like themselves; that he would compromise, make deals. They did not understand that Hitler was not an ordinary politician, that he had revolutionary plans, for himself and for Germany. And they did not anticipate that Hitler planned to establish a dictatorship! According to the Weimar Constitution, which was still in force, Hitler would need a two-thirds majority in the Reichstag to change the constitution. His opponents, such as the Social Democrats, believed he would never control so many votes.

Their mistake was to believe that Hitler intended to govern within the legal system. Five years earlier Joseph Goebbels had explained the Nazi attitude to democratic rule:

> We enter the Reichstag, that arsenal of democracy, so as to help ourselves to its own weapons. We become Reichstag deputies in order to cripple the Weimar mentality with its own crutches. If democracy is stupid enough to provide us with free travel and attendance allowances in return for this work of demolition, that's its own affair. . . . So long as it's legal we don't mind what means we use to revolutionize the present state of affairs. . . . If in these elections we succeed in planting some sixty or seventy agitators from our party in the various parliaments, our fighting machine will thereafter be state-

*Following Hitler's appointment as Chancellor, the Nazi Party in Berlin staged this parade. Events such as this became a familiar sight in Germany during the 1930s.*

*equipped and state-subsidized. . . . No one should imagine that parliamentarianism will tame us. . . . We come as enemies! As a wolf irrupts into a flock of sheep, so too will we. Now ye have strangers in your midst!*

Once in power, Hitler demonstrated the truth of Goebbel's remarks.

Within weeks of his appointment, Hitler persuaded President Hindenburg to call new elections. No party, including the National Socialists, had solid control of the Reichstag; Hitler wanted a chance to increase the Nazis' number of seats. At the same time, he invoked emergency powers which the Weimar Constitution granted to every Chancellor. He issued a decree "for the protection of the German people" which gave him power to control the press and political meetings. These were only initial steps, but they revealed Hitler's intentions to concentrate political power in his own hands. His opponents, however, did not understand their full significance so they did not try to stop them. Vice-Chancellor Papen, who was not a follower of Hitler's, did not protest these regulations either. He and his conservative colleagues were not willing to defend the Weimar Constitution because they, too, like Hitler, were fed up with democracy.

## THE REICHSTAG FIRE

Near the end of February, barely a week before new elections were to be held, an event occurred in Berlin that has generated much controversy: the Reichstag building was badly damaged in a fire. Historians still dispute whether or not the Nazis themselves actually planned the fire, but there is no argument over their cynical exploitation of the event.

By most accounts, the fire was set by Marinus van der Lubbe, a twenty-four-year-old native of Holland who hoped to arouse the workers of Germany against Hitler. As soon as Hitler learned of the fire, he blamed the communists. Van der Lubbe did have communist sympathies, but he was not a member of the Communist Party. There was no evidence that party members, let alone communist deputies in the Reichstag, were part of a conspiracy to burn the parliament building. But Hitler used the fire to his own advantage. Claiming the communists were trying to overthrow the government, he pushed through a state of emergency which suspended civil liberties protected by the Weimar Constitution—free speech, free press, the right to be secure in one's own home, the right to assemble and form organizations. Then, within a few days, three thousand communists and Social Democrats were picked up throughout the country by the police, who, by this time, were under the orders of Hitler's men.

All this occurred just days before the new elections. Hitler and his Nazi colleagues thrived in this atmosphere of crisis. Playing on the public's fear of a revolution directed by the Soviet Union, Hitler insisted that only the Nazis, through their determined, patriotic efforts, could successfully oppose the communists. And the Nazis made very plain the tactics they would use against the communists and all other opponents. Hermann Göring, who was in Hitler's cabinet and who also served as Interior Minister of Prussia, Germany's largest and most influential state, was not afraid to explain himself clearly. Speaking to voters in Frankfurt two days before the election, he said: "Fellow Germans, my measures will not be crippled by any judicial thinking . . . I won't have to worry about justice, my mission is only to destroy and exterminate. This struggle will be a struggle against chaos, and I shall conduct it with police power."

The Nazis' campaign won the support of rich industrialists who feared communist rule would deprive them of ownership of their factories. Large firms like Krupp and I. G. Farben contributed millions of marks (which equaled hundreds of thousands of dollars), making it possible for Goebbels to organize a massive campaign in support of Adolf Hitler. Even so, the Nazis received only 43.9 percent of the votes in the election; Hitler would still need the support of other parties to gain a majority in the Reichstag. But he was not discouraged. He knew that total power was within his grasp and he intended to seize it, with or without democratic methods.

## THE ENABLING ACT

The newly elected Reichstag opened on March 21 with an impressive ceremony staged by Goebbels. It was held in a church in Potsdam, an old city just southwest of Berlin. Both Hitler and President Hindenburg attended. Hitler paid homage to the old man, giving the impression that his aims were moderate. This was a standard technique of his, especially once he became Chancellor. He liked to camouflage his radical intentions behind reasonable-sounding rhetoric. Two days later Hitler spoke more boldly.

The Reichstag was now meeting temporarily in a large Berlin opera house. This meeting of the parliament was the first to be dominated by the Nazis. Hermann Göring served as its President. A large swastika flag hung behind the speaker's podium while Nazi stormtroopers patrolled halls in the building. Then Adolf Hitler entered the hall. His supporters greeted him with shouts and upraised right arms—the Nazi salute to their Führer. This was Hitler's first appearance before the Reichstag. His speech sounded moderate, reassuring. He promised to respect private property. He vowed to help farmers and middle-class families. He would find means to end unemployment and nurture peaceful relations with Germany's old enemies: England, France, and even Russia.

There was nothing surprising in these goals and certainly nothing objectionable, but to accomplish them Hitler asked the Reichstag to enact the Law for Alleviating the Distress of People and Reich. This law, now remembered as the Enabling

Members of the Reichstag gathered in this church in
Potsdam to hear the new Chancellor, Adolf Hitler,
pay homage to the aging President, Paul von Hindenburg.

Act, would grant Hitler the power to change laws and even to alter the constitution. Hitler was, indeed, asking for extraordinary power. Nevertheless, the Reichstag was intimidated into approving the Enabling Act, 441 to 94, thereby destroying itself. Only the Social Democrats opposed him. Adolf Hitler became the source of law and justice in Germany. Outwardly, Hitler's use of the Reichstag to gain overriding power gave his actions the appearance of legality. But in reality, he was just using the parliament to effect his own revolution.

Within four months, German politics were completely transformed. In May 1933 Hitler's men arrested the country's labor leaders, sending them to concentration camps which the Nazis had constructed that spring. In June Hitler began to outlaw political parties. First, the Social Democratic Party was banned, then the State and German People's parties were outlawed. The Catholic Center Party dissolved itself. Even Hitler's ally, the German National Party, was thrown out of existence. By the middle of July the National Socialist German Workers' Party was the only legal political party in Germany. Like the Bolsheviks in Russia, the Nazis believed in one-party rule that tolerated no opposition. The Weimar Republic was now extinguished.

HITLER'S PURGE OF THE SA

While Hitler was taking care of natural opponents, he neglected elements within the Nazi movement who favored a more radical social revolution for Germany. The SA or stormtroopers, led by Captain Ernst Rohm, had played an important role in the development of the party. They were the Nazi stalwarts who protected Hitler at meetings and challenged communists in the streets. By the time Hitler came to power in 1933 the SA numbered nearly three million members. Rohm believed his men deserved not only responsibility for internal security but also responsibility for the country's defense.

This was Rohm's downfall. He did not understand that Hitler needed the support of the German generals to rebuild the armed forces into a unified war machine. These generals, however, resented Rohm and his expectations for the SA: they were not about to share their role in defending Germany or in training the country's young men for war.

Hitler tried to arrange a compromise. He agreed to allow certain SA units to serve along the nation's borders and he also assigned the SA the task of organizing preliminary military training for young men aged eighteen to twenty-one. Outwardly, Rohm accepted these terms, but in reality he was angered by this diminished role. He continued to insist on the SA's importance, claiming in one speech that "The SA *is* the National Socialist Revolution!"

Rohm did not intend to overthrow Hitler, but his activity and the growth of the SA disturbed other leading Nazis, like Hermann Göring, who was president of the Reichstag and Minister of the Interior for Prussia; General Reinhard Heydrich, the head of the Nazi's internal security police; and Heinrich Himmler, the head of the Gestapo, the feared secret police. These three men now headed important agencies. They felt threatened by Rohm and by the size of his SA, and they were loyal to Adolf Hitler above everything. They decided to trap Rohm by convincing Hitler that Rohm was planning a revolt. Hitler would have no choice but to stop him.

Hitler still hesitated. He felt loyal to Rohm and he wanted to avoid an open conflict with the SA. But Hitler was also under pressure from numerous quarters. His Vice-Chancellor, Franz von Papen, despised Rohm. Papen was a favorite of the army, and in turn, he sided with the generals in their dispute with Rohm. If Hitler refused to deal with the SA, Papen intended to ask Hindenburg, who was still President, to remove Hitler from power and have the military take over the country. In addition to Papen's opposition, Heydrich and Göring would not allow the matter to rest. They arranged false documents and spread rumors to persuade Hitler and the army that Rohm really did intend to lead a revolt. Events came to a climax near the end of June 1934.

According to Hitler's biographer, John Toland, on the morning of June 30 Hitler himself led a small group of armed men to a hotel in southern Germany where Rohm was on vacation. Barely past dawn, Hitler, revolver in hand, awoke Rohm and personally announced his arrest. At the same time, other leaders of the SA, in Berlin and Munich, as well as in other cities, were arrested.

Göring took charge of the purge in Berlin. Under his direction and with the approval of Hitler, the Gestapo rounded up the SA leadership and also attacked previous opponents of Hitler. General Kurt von Schleicher and his wife were murdered in their home. Vice-Chancellor Franz von Papen's press officer was shot. Several generals were assassinated. Gregor Strasser, who had remained loyal to Hitler, was also killed because Goebbels and Göring remembered him as an enemy.

In Bavaria Hitler issued orders for the execution of several SA leaders. At first, Hans Frank, the Bavarian Minister of Justice, hesitated to approve the executions. He was a lawyer and he wanted procedures to conform with the law. But Hitler insisted on his right to order execution, with or without trials.

With regard to Rohm, however, even Hitler was confused. He did not want to kill him. Rohm was one of his veteran followers. They had gone through many difficulties together, including the failed Putsch in 1923. Hitler felt close to him personally, as well. But if Rohm were not shot, how could Hitler justify the massacre of others who were far less important in this alleged revolt? Hitler hesitated for a day, then ordered Rohm executed in his cell.

The purge of the SA and the violent attacks on other political figures marked a turning point in Hitler's program. Up until then he had tried not to upset his conservative allies or the army. As long as the Nazis attacked liberals, Jews, socialists, and communists, conservative politicians did not object. Even the purge of the SA itself would have been tolerated. Vice-Chancellor von Papen had, after all, called upon Hitler to limit Rohm's authority. But General von Schleicher had once served as Chancellor of Germany. Surely his fellow officers would protest his murder! Few came forward. The German army was too satisfied to see Rohm dead to bother about legal procedure or even von Schleicher's assassination.

The purge involved a violent and illegal series of executions, but neither the army nor any other important segment of German society protested. The cabinet endorsed Hitler's action unanimously, giving him, a license to execute.

Within eighteen months of reaching power, Hitler had gained control of all the important sectors of German society. Each time he made a move, against the trade unions, other political parties, the SA, or even elements in the army, he received the approval of the Reichstag. Through political persuasion and outright violence, Hitler could now look at Germany and believe, with a good deal of evidence, that the country was united behind him. He could now set out to conquer Europe.

## RE-ARMAMENT

When Adolf Hitler came to power in 1933 Germany was a weak country. Her army, the Reichswehr, was limited to one hundred thousand men, and her naval and air capabilities were very small. Under the terms of the Versailles treaty, the Rhineland was still demilitarized. Yet Hitler was not discouraged. Ever since the German defeat in 1918 he had been determined to reverse his country's humiliation. Now that he had complete power inside Germany, he turned his gaze across its borders.

Although in *Mein Kampf* Hitler had proclaimed his aggressive dreams, once he became Chancellor he declared that his intentions were peaceful, that Germany only sought to defend itself against the threat of communism. In a speech to the Reichstag on May 17, 1933, he explained himself this way:

> *Germany has disarmed. All the terms imposed upon her by the treaty have been fulfilled, and fulfilled far beyond the call of justice, if not beyond the call of reason. . . . Should all nations agree to a universal and international control of armaments, Germany would always be prepared to submit to inspection. . . . in order that the whole world might have irrefutable proof of her wholly unmilitary character. . . . These demands do not imply rearmament but rather our desire that other countries should disarm. . . . The only nation having good reason to fear invasion is the German nation which has not only been denied offensive weapons but whose entitlement to weapons of defense has actually been curtailed, while the construction of frontier defenses has been forbidden her. . . . Germany is concerned not with aggression but with security.*

By 1935 many people in France and England recognized that the Versailles treaty had been terribly unfair to Germany. So they were sympathetic to Hitler's desire to restore German honor and the country's right to self-defense. In March, Hitler began negotiations with the British and French over increasing the size of Germany's armed forces. The talks were held in Berlin; Great Britain was represented by her ambassador Sir Eric Phipps, Anthony Eden, who became Foreign Secretary in December, and Sir John Simon, England's Foreign

One of Hitler's chief goals on assuming power was
to rebuild the German army into a powerful fighting
force that no country in Europe would oppose. Here he
is seen reviewing troops with Heinrich Himmler.

Secretary at the time. The French ambassador Andrei François-Pônçet also took part.

Hitler was an effective negotiator. Anthony Eden was impressed by Hitler's intelligence. He later commented that Hitler participated "without hesitation and without notes, as befitted the man who knew where he wanted to go." Hitler argued on behalf of German interests in a calm and polite manner that surprised the British. But he could also lose his composure when an issue angered him, moving from the pose of reasonable statesman to aroused fanatic. Nonetheless, Hitler got what he wanted, asking for an air force no larger than sixty percent of the French air force. How aggressive could he be? He expanded the army from a hundred thousand to three hundred thousand men. He built up the navy to thirty-five percent of Great Britain's tonnage.

Hitler re-armed Germany gradually. He did not want to alarm the western powers. As he told his generals just four days after coming to power: "The most dangerous period will be during the reconstruction of the armed forces. Then we shall see whether or not France possesses any statesmen; if she does she'll give us no time and fall on us instead." But the French were reluctant to oppose Hitler directly. Sensing their hesitation, he took the initiative.

Ever since 1918 Germany had been deprived of full military sovereignty because it was not permitted to have troops in the Rhineland, an area along Germany's border with France. To prevent war, the Versailles treaty forbade the stationing of German troops in an area thirty miles to the east of the river as well as on all German territory on the western side, between the French border and the river itself. This arrangement left Germany defenseless. Now Hitler decided to challenge the French. His generals urged caution. If the French decided to act, they could immediately invade the Rhineland from the west, exposing the Germans as weak and vulnerable. Hitler preferred to gamble.

On Saturday morning, March 7, 1936, three infantry battalions of German troops crossed the Rhine River over six bridges. Foreign reporters gathered in Cologne to watch some of the troops on the move. The soldiers were under orders to withdraw—fighting—if the French took action. By Monday more than twenty-five thousand German troops were in the Rhineland. Hitler was under tremendous strain. He knew, he told one colleague, that if the French attacked "we would have had to withdraw with our tails between our legs, for the military resources at our disposal would have been wholly inadequate for even a moderate resistance." It soon was evident, though, that Hitler had gotten his way. The French protested vigorously, but they did not challenge Germany's forces in the Rhineland with troops of their own. Hitler drew an obvious and tragic conclusion. He saw that by using force he could make the French and British, who were afraid of another war, back down.

Events in other parts of the world reinforced Hitler's belief that the western democracies would not stand up to him. In Italy the dictator Benito Mussolini had been in power since 1922. He was the leader of the Italian Fascist Party, which, like the Nazis, glorified force as a means to gain and hold onto power. Mussolini also had imperial dreams. He wanted to restore the glory of the ancient Roman empire to modern Italy. In 1935 Mussolini invaded Abyssinia (the present country of Ethiopia), a poor, undeveloped kingdom in northern Africa. The major governments denounced Italy for its action but no effective measures were taken to halt Italian aggression. And in Spain a revolt by right-wing military officers in 1936, led by General Francisco Franco, threatened the Spanish republic. Mussolini and Hitler sent planes and other supplies to aid Franco while the western democracies maintained an official policy of nonintervention. Once again Hitler could see that neither France nor England was willing to do more than offer sympathy.

## ANSCHLUSS, THE UNION OF
## GERMANY AND AUSTRIA

In this international climate, Hitler planned his next move. This time his target was Austria. After World War I and the breakup of the Austro-Hungarian Empire, Vienna had become the capital of an independent, German-speaking Austria in the heart of Central Europe. Hitler dreamed of *Anschluss*, the union of Austria, the place of his birth, with Germany itself. Italy, under Mussolini, regarded itself as the protector of Austrian independence, but with Italy's growing cooperation with Germany, Hitler hoped that Mussolini would not interfere with his plans for Austria.

Already in 1934 Germany was putting pressure on Austria. Hitler gave moral and financial support to Austrian Nazis who carried out terrorist activities, such as blowing up railroad tracks and electric power stations. That summer a small group of Austrian Nazis attempted a revolt, hoping to capture Austrian Chancellor Engelbert Dollfuss and other members of his cabinet. The revolt failed but not before Dollfuss was murdered, shot in the throat by the Nazis. Embarrassed by the plot, the Nazis retreated.

For a time, Hitler smoothed over his differences with Austria. He asked Franz von Papen, who once served as German Chancellor and was Hitler's Vice-Chancellor for two years, to go to Vienna as Germany's ambassador. In February 1938, however, Papen was recalled to Germany. He went immediately to Berchtesgaden, Hitler's isolated villa near the German-Austrian border not far from Salzburg. There, talking with Hitler, Papen convinced him to meet personally with Austrian Chancellor Kurt von Schuschnigg in order to resolve their differences.

Schuschnigg accepted Hitler's invitation and came to Berchtesgaden on February 12. Hitler spoke aggressively, accusing Austria of fortifying their common border. ''You don't seriously believe you can stop me or even delay me for half an hour, do you?'' Hitler told him. Then Hitler gave Schuschnigg his demands. First, Austria must release all imprisoned Nazis, including the assassins of Chancellor Dollfuss. Second, a Nazi sympathizer named Artur Seyss-Inquart should be made Minister of Interior, with full control over Austria's police forces. Third, Hitler wanted a Nazi to be Austria's Minister of Defense.

Schuschnigg understood that Hitler's demands put a virtual end to Austria's sovereignty. He could not accept them on his own authority anyway; they would have to be ratified by Austrian President Wilhelm Miklas. Hitler flew into a rage. He dismissed Schuschnigg and shouted for General Wilhelm Keitel to come to his study. This was meant to intimidate Schuschnigg by making it seem as if Hitler were planning an immediate military attack. Schuschnigg thought he might be arrested. When he saw Hitler later that day, though, Hitler had made a sudden shift in approach. He offered Schuschnigg three days to gain approval in Vienna. Schuschnigg accepted the compromise and signed the agreement. Then he returned to Vienna.

While Schuschnigg discussed the agreement with President Miklas, Hitler had his army carry out maneuvers along the border. This military threat, as well as Hitler's behavior in Berchtesgaden, intimidated the Austrian government. By February 14 it accepted all of Hitler's demands. But Hitler still did not have what he wanted: *Anschluss*, the full integration of Austria into the German Reich. New pressures were exerted on Austria. Hitler wanted fuller economic ties between Austria and Germany. He demanded that a Nazi be appointed Minister of Finance and that the Nazi party, which was still banned in Austria, be made legal.

Schuschnigg was determined to save Austria. On March 8, he announced a plebiscite to take place five days later. The Austrian people would be asked one question: ''Are you in favor of a free and German, independent and social, Christian and united Austria?'' A vote "yes" meant opposition both to Hitler and to German domination of Austria.

Hitler could not tolerate this defiance. If Schuschnigg got his way, the plebiscite could put an end to Hitler's hopes for *Anschluss*. So he mobilized German troops, demanding the plebiscite be postponed. Once again, Austria was compelled to back down. Schuschnigg tried to rally support from England and France, but British Prime Minister Neville Chamberlain, in particular, did not want to oppose Hitler. He adopted a policy of appeasement, hoping to satisfy Hitler's demands and avoid war. (Anthony Eden, Britain's Foreign Secretary, resigned in protest over Chamberlain's policy of appeasement.) Without allies, Schuschnigg knew it would be foolish to challenge Hitler. Germany was larger and stronger; Hitler was prepared to invade. So Schuschnigg resigned, leaving the Nazis able to maneuver Seyss-Inquart into power as Austrian Chancellor.

German troops entered Austria on March 12. They were greeted as friends by most of the population. Hitler, too, visited Austria on that Saturday, stopping in cities like Lambach and Linz where he had grown up. Hitler's stormtroopers were close behind the regular army, and they behaved in Austria as they did inside Germany, particularly in their treatment of the Jewish population. Jews were dragged from their homes and offices and molested in the streets. Schuschnigg's plebiscite, originally scheduled for March 10, was not forgotten in the rush of military occupation. Postponed until April 10, the vote was nearly unanimous in favor of *Anschluss*.

Hitler's prestige rose even higher in Germany. As in the Rhineland, he showed he was able to get what he wanted without shedding blood, primarily because the principal western powers, England and France, were not willing to challenge him.

Although Hitler had every reason to remain confident in his policies, his health was causing him great concern. Hitler saw himself as Germany's savior, but he believed he had to hurry to accomplish his goals before death shortened his career. His mother's death from cancer had affected him profoundly, and he began to fear that he would also die of cancer. He often told his closest colleagues that he did not expect to live a long life. Shortly after *Anschluss*, one of Hitler's greatest triumphs, he drew up his will. By 1938 he had a large personal fortune, mostly from the royalties of *Mein Kampf*. In the will he named Eva Braun, his two sisters, and his brother among his beneficiaries. The Nazi party was to receive his personal possessions in the event of his death.

## CZECHOSLOVAKIA

With Austria and Germany united, Hitler was now in a position to alter significantly the balance of forces in Europe. He was especially interested in gaining territory in the east, in Poland and the Soviet Union, to give Germany "living space" or *lebensraum*, as he called it in *Mein Kampf*. But first he needed to have Czechoslovakia, which lay directly in his path to Poland and the Soviet Union. Hitler was prepared to use force but he got his way once again without calling on the army.

Soon after the absorption of Austria into the Reich, a group of ethnic Germans living in Czechoslovakia began demanding a similar arrangement. They were called Sudeten Germans and their leader, Konrad Heinlein, was a Nazi. This German-speaking minority within Czechoslovakia was not being mistreated, but they claimed they were and they hoped to create enough tension and unrest in Czechoslovakia to justify an invasion by Hitler in order to "save" them.

The Czechs, led by President Eduard Beneš, were willing to resist German domination. They had strong military defenses and also believed that England and France as well as the Soviet Union would not allow Germany to invade without coming to Czechoslovakia's defense. But Beneš was mistaken. Prime Minister Chamberlain was prepared to sacrifice Czechoslovakia, just as he had Austria, hoping finally to satisfy Hitler. He wrote his sister that "you only have to look at a map to see that nothing that France or we could do, could possibly save Czechoslovakia from being overrun by the Germans."

The crisis over Czechoslovakia lasted more than half a year. Many people feared that war would break out in May 1938. Czech troops were mobilized while France intended to mobilize her army as well if Germany marched on Czechoslovakia. But Hitler was only starting to devise his plan. He ordered his generals to prepare an invasion of Czechoslovakia. He spoke calmly to them, making it clear that Czechoslovakia was only an intermediate step on the road to war with Poland and Russia.

His generals were not happy with the idea of invading Czechoslovakia, a move that would bring Germany face to face with England, France, and America. These countries, in addition to Czechoslovakia and the Soviet Union, possessed resources that were superior to Germany's. The generals remembered the disasters of World War I, the war on two fronts that, in the end, humiliated Germany. Hitler, however, was sure that neither France nor England would react with arms.

By fall, political tension in Central Europe was enormous. War seemed inevitable. Sudeten Germans were demonstrating in support of Hitler, creating disorders and riots—just the kind of provocation Hitler needed in order "to save them." But the Czechs were not intimidated. Prime Minister Neville Chamberlain, realizing that a general European war could break out if Germany attacked Czechoslovakia, offered to talk with Hitler personally.

Chamberlain traveled to Germany on September 15, 1938. He and Hitler spoke for three hours, alone with Hitler's interpreter, in a study at Berchtesgaden. Hitler expressed himself forcefully, insisting he was ready to use his army. Chamberlain did not back down. "If that is so," he asked Hitler, "why did you let me come to Berchtesgaden?" Then Chamberlain declared his readiness to leave. This startled Hitler. He asked how Chamberlain regarded the situation of the Sudeten Germans. Chamberlain was willing to cede the Sudetenland to Germany, but he could not agree without consulting the French and the Czechs themselves. He also offered to meet Hitler in Germany a second time.

On his return to London, Chamberlain conferred with French leaders, both sides agreeing that Czechoslovakia should cede the Sudetenland to Germany as the only alternative to war. President Beneš tried to resist the proposal, but finding no ally to help him, he gave in.

Chamberlain returned to Germany a second time on September 22. With the Czechs ready to give up the Sudetenland, Chamberlain thought he could now satisfy Hitler. But Hitler, always pressing for more, demanded that German troops be allowed to occupy the Sudetenland immediately. While Chamberlain could not agree to this, he succeeded in getting the Czechs to approve a new timetable, allowing Germany to move in within ten days. When Chamberlain returned to England from Munich, he received a hero's welcome. He sincerely believed he had secured "peace for our time." And he also believed Hitler's promise that Czechoslovakia was "his last territorial demand in Europe."

The Munich Conference marked the last step in the British and French policy of appeasement. For Hitler it was a diplomatic triumph. For Czechoslovakia it was a national disaster. In England most people wanted to applaud Chamberlain's efforts, but Winston Churchill warned: "We have sustained a great defeat without a war, the consequences of which will travel far with us . . . and do not suppose that this is the end. This is only the beginning of the reckoning."

Churchill understood Hitler far better than Chamberlain did. Hitler's successes between 1936 and 1939 made him seem invincible. He had re-armed Germany, moved his troops into the Rhineland, and gained control of Austria and Czechoslovakia, all by bluff and diplomatic maneuvers. His dreams were being fulfilled. Poland became his next goal.

By the spring of 1939, however, the western powers had run out of patience. Both England and France made solemn pledges to declare war on Germany if Poland were invaded. Hitler was confident he could defeat them but he wondered if they would really fight. After all, they had not lifted a finger to protect Austria or Czechoslovakia. Why should Poland be different?

In the event that England and France to his west did decide to fight, Hitler wanted to avoid major fighting in the east. To the world's surprise, he was able to arrange a non-aggression pact with the Soviet Union. Hitler and Joseph Stalin, the Soviet dictator, never met each other; negotiations were carried out by their foreign ministers, Joachim von Ribbentrop and Vyacheslav Molotov. Stalin had his own reasons for signing an agreement with Hitler. He knew the Soviet Union was not ready for war, and he hoped to gain time to prepare for a conflict. Stalin also believed that Germany would not attack the Soviet Union once the treaty was signed.

The Ribbentrop-Molotov pact was a triumph for Hitler. For two years, between 1939 and 1941, while German armies overran Western Europe and Poland, the Soviet Union supplied Germany with strategic materials and allowed Japan to transport goods to Germany across Soviet military lines. Having forestalled a war on two fronts, Hitler was confident of victory when German troops crossed the Polish border on September 1, 1939.

World War II had begun.

# DESTRUCTION

# 4

World War II was the most extensive and destructive conflict in human history. Many aspects of the war are difficult to comprehend. Its scale alone—the fact that armies clashed over several continents and oceans, involving tens of millions of soldiers—was unprecedented. New machines of war—airplanes, tanks, submarines, aircraft carriers—were used for the first time as principal means of attack. In previous wars governments had concentrated their efforts on destroying each other's armed forces, but in World War II both the Axis powers—Germany and Japan—and the Allies—the United States, Great Britain, and the Soviet Union—bombarded cities, leaving millions of civilians dead, disabled, and homeless.

By 1939 Adolf Hitler had sole responsibility for Germany's domestic and foreign policy. He was head of state and Supreme Commander of the German army. Once the war began, he personally directed every aspect of the conflict, planning Germany's economic, military, and political strategies. But though Hitler assumed these enormous responsibilities and was for a time more successful than he himself ever

*Hitler confers with his staff officers behind
the lines in Poland in September, 1939.*

dreamed, Germany's eventual defeat reflected, in part, Hitler's own inadequacies as a wartime leader.

Adolf Hitler had a unique ability to command the loyalty of people around him. Much of this authority came with his successes. Despite his generals' hesitation, he had been able to defy England and France between 1934 and 1939, restore German prestige, and gain enormous territory. The Polish campaign confirmed Germany's military revival. In a coordinated land and air attack, German troops destroyed the Polish air force and most of its army. As Hitler planned, his new tactic of *blitzkrieg* or lightning war overwhelmed Poland within four weeks.

Hitler closely followed the German advance into Poland. He rode to the front in an open car while his subordinates tossed packs of cigarettes to the soldiers. But Hitler would not visit the wounded. He did not like to see suffering with his own eyes.

Adolf Hitler did not believe that his attack on Poland would start a general European conflict. In a secret memorandum to the Hitler-Stalin pact, in August, 1939 Germany and the Soviet Union had agreed to divide Poland. And though England and France declared war on Germany right after the invasion of Poland, Hitler still thought he could avoid war with England. England was a maritime power which, he hoped, would not fight over problems in continental Europe.

In October, Hitler made speeches questioning the need for war in the west. At the same time, though, he developed plans to attack France. The winter of 1939 passed quietly on the western front while Germany prepared its offensive. The generals proposed attacking through northern France and Belgium, just as Germany had advanced in World War I. But Hitler would not accept such a familiar plan. He preferred to concentrate the attack on the northern flank of the western front, invading Luxembourg, Belgium, and Holland. Hitler's plan called for bypassing France's formidable defense arrangement, the Maginot Line. His generals did not have confidence in this plan, except for General Erich von Manstein who, independently of Hitler, drew up a similar plan of attack.

## THE COLLAPSE OF EUROPE

The offensive began on May 10. Hitler helped prepare the details, even briefing a group of soldiers who were to capture Belgian fortresses in a surprise attack with the use of gliders. The German offensive caught England and France off-guard. Within a week, the French knew they were beaten. By May 19 the Nazis had trapped the remnants of the Belgian army, the entire British Expeditionary Force, and three French armies. No one expected France to fall so quickly. In England, Neville Chamberlain was forced to resign and Winston Churchill became Prime Minister.

The British faced a terrible defeat. An army of British and Allied troops was trapped on the beaches of Dunkirk, an industrial French city on the North Sea coast. Hitler could have allowed his infantry and artillery units to capture the city, thereby closing the last possible route of escape for the British. But instead he let Göring convince him to order the Luftwaffe, the German air force, to attack the British on the beaches. The plan failed. German bombs sank too deeply into the sand, muffling their explosive effect. Meanwhile, the British sent thousands of boats across the Channel and managed to rescue more than three hundred thousand soldiers.

It is hard to know why Hitler permitted the British to escape. His infantry could still have attacked once it was clear that Göring's bombers were not succeeding. But he restrained his forces. Perhaps he was still hoping the British would not fight Germany, that they would remain neutral or even support his plan to attack Russia, whenever that occurred. He may have permitted the British to escape in order to preserve the possibility of future German-British cooperation.

In any case, Hitler appeared to be invincible. His armies conquered with ease. Poland had fallen in four weeks, now Norway fell in eight. Holland was defeated in five days, Belgium in seventeen. Hitler took France in six weeks, Yugoslavia in eleven days, and Greece in three weeks. Twenty-five years earlier, he had fought as a mere corporal, surviving trench warfare while receiving six medals, including the Iron Cross, First Class. Now he was the undisputed leader of the German armed forces.

Hitler's experiences in World War I had taught him significant lessons. He wanted to avoid drawn-out, stationary fighting. Trench warfare had been a disaster for Germany. The other countries also had greater material resources. So Hitler developed a *blitzkrieg* strategy, hoping to defeat his opponents one at a time in rapid order. He also wanted to avoid a two-front war, a conflict he knew Germany could not win. So he forestalled this development by making peace with Russia before invading Poland and then France.

By the summer of 1940 his plans had succeeded so well that it is necessary to ask why he continued to fight. Germany controlled virtually all of Europe up to the Soviet border. Great Britain remained a strong maritime power but it was no threat to Germany on the continent. Stalin was proving to be a reliable ally. Strategic material continued to pour into Germany from the U.S.S.R., and Stalin allowed German ships in the North Sea to dock at Murmansk for repairs. He also provided news of weather conditions, helping the German air force plan attacks on England.

If Hitler had stopped hostilities in 1940, after the fall of France, he would have been the greatest European conqueror in history, greater even than Napoleon. But he could not restrain himself. He knew that in the west, England would never accept German domination of Europe. And he feared that in the east, Stalin would wait until the Soviet Union was stronger and then attack the Reich at an opportune moment. Hitler had created an enormous army. He had proclaimed National Socialism the avowed enemy of communism. With almost all of Europe under his control he could not restrain himself from seeking one of his ultimate goals: the destruction of the Soviet Union. It proved to be a fatal mistake. As Napoleon once remarked, "The most dangerous moment comes with victory."

With German armies in control of France, Hitler hoped to invade England before turning his gaze to Russia. His generals prepared an invasion plan—Operation Sea Lion—but the British had the most formidable navy in the world. The English Channel, too, with its rough seas and unpredictable weather, made a military crossing difficult to achieve. Hitler therefore ordered his air force—the Luftwaffe—to soften England's willingness to resist.

When the air offensive began on August 13, England was ready. Two years earlier the British secret intelligence service, named MI-6, had bought the secret of a German cipher machine. With this information the Allies were able to decode German communications. When the Luftwaffe attacked, the Royal Air Force was waiting for them. Although they were outnumbered, the British Spitfires wreaked havoc on the slower German Stuka dive bombers. The Battle of Britain was won in the air. There were days in August when the Germans lost more than seventy planes while the British force lost about thirty. By September Hitler ordered mass raids on London. On one day alone, the Nazis sent three hundred twenty bombers across the Channel. But the British, led by Winston Churchill and Air Marshal Sir Hugh Dowding, held fast. Hitler gave in and abandoned the idea of crossing the Channel. Instead he turned east to the Soviet Union.

## BARBAROSSA, WAR WITH
## THE SOVIET UNION

Hitler decided on his own to invade the Soviet Union. His generals cautioned him. They understood that with England still free there was always a chance that a second front could be opened in the west. But Hitler ignored their advice. He personally directed the invasion plans, named Barbarossa. He imposed strict secrecy on his staff, not even telling his ally Mussolini or the German Ambassador in Moscow about Barbarossa. Hitler assembled the most massive military force in history: over 4,000,000 men, 3,500 tanks, 3,900 planes, and 50,000 pieces of artillery.

Hitler's nerve and timing outsmarted Stalin. The Soviet dictator ignored his own intelligence reports that a Nazi invasion was imminent. One Soviet spy, Richard Sorge who was based in Tokyo, even supplied Stalin with the invasion date: June 22, 1941. Stalin ignored this warning also, with disastrous results.

The Red Army collapsed along the whole 930-mile front. Within six months, about four million Soviet soldiers were captured and three million were killed. Most of the Ukraine, including Kiev, was occupied, Leningrad was besieged, and Moscow itself was threatened. In November, barely five months after the invasion, Soviet troops paraded through Red Square on the anniversary of the Bolshevik revolution and then marched to the front; the Germans were near the suburbs.

This was the most destructive fighting in the war. The Russians lost at least 20,000,000 people, over 1,700 towns and cities, and with them 32,000 factories and 70,000 villages. Parts of the Ukraine and Byelorussia were occupied for three years, during which time the Germans shot over one million Jews. Leningrad remained under seige for nine hundred days. Almost half the city's population, well over a million people, perished, mostly from hunger. There were incidents of cannibalism.

With the occupation of large parts of the Soviet Union, the Nazis found themselves controlling the centers of Jewish life in Europe. Poland, Lithuania, the Ukraine, and Byelorussia contained millions of Jews. Jews had lived in Poland for more than a thousand years. By the 1930s Poland's three and a half million Jews made up one-tenth of the country's population. Aside from a large group of traditional, religious Jews, there was a thriving secular Jewish life, with theaters and magazines, political parties and Zionist organizations. As low as his opinion was of Germany's Jews, Hitler regarded these "Eastern Jews" as the most inferior of peoples, and now that he controlled them, he had to decide what to do with them.

Already in the initial years of Nazi rule, German Jews had faced new and severe treatment. In April 1933, barely two months after coming to power, the Nazis organized a boycott of business establishments owned by Jews. Stormtroopers stood outside stores for three days asking customers to shop elsewhere. On April 7 Hitler removed Jews from civil service

*This sign on a closed shop warns:*
*"Germans! Defend yourselves!*
*Do not buy from Jews!"*
*A Nazi stormtrooper stands by*
*to enforce the boycott that*
*marked the beginning of Hitler's*
*anti-Semitic policies.*

posts. A few weeks later he gained approval of the Law Against Overcrowding of German Schools, limiting the number of Jewish students in schools of higher education. This was only the beginning of his anti-Semitic measures.

On September 15, 1935, the Reichstag passed the infamous "Nuremberg Laws," named after the city in which Hitler announced them: the Reich Citizenship Law and the Law for the Protection of German Blood and German Honor. The first reduced the Jews to second-class citizenship, taking away their protections under law. The second outlawed marriages between Jews and non-Jews because, as the Nazis explained, "an acute danger threatened the German people from Jewry alone, the law aims primarily at the prevention of further mixing of blood with Jews."

Under this kind of pressure, Jews in large numbers left Germany. Many came to the United States, and many others went to Palestine, where Jews from Eastern Europe had been moving since the 1880s to escape anti-Semitism. Here in the ancient land of Israel, a small, barren strip of land along the eastern edge of the Mediterranean Sea, they wanted to build a new society where Jews could be secure. Thousands of German Jews began arriving in Palestine in the 1930s. But many remained behind, unable to appreciate that Hitler was not an ordinary anti-Semite.

CRYSTAL NIGHT

The first large-scale physical attack on Jews occurred in November 1938. Until that time spontaneous groups of anti-Semites had attacked Jews and synagogues, but they were not officially directed by the government. This policy changed in November. On November 7, 1938, a young Jew named Herschel Grynszpan killed Ernst von Rath, a minor German embassy official in Paris. Grynszpan's parents had been deported from Germany to Poland. Distressed by their plight and the growing pressure on the Jews of Germany, Grynszpan intended to kill the German Ambassador but instead shot von Rath. Within two days there were riots throughout Germany. Hitler made it clear that the police were not to discourage attacks on Jewish neighborhoods. Goebbels and other party leaders understood this meant that wholesale attacks could be mounted.

Uniformed Nazis burned nearly two hundred synagogues and ransacked Jewish neighborhoods, destroying over seven thousand shops owned by Jews. It came to be called Crystal Night because of all the broken glass in the street. Scores of Jews were also killed or wounded. There were protests throughout the world but the Nazis reacted cynically, blaming the Jews themselves for the destruction and requiring the Jewish community to pay for the damage.

## THE FINAL SOLUTION

From the beginning of his career, Hitler had placed the Jewish question at the center of his mental universe. The Jews were his chief enemy. While still in Landsberg prison, Hitler already had in mind what he would do to the Jews if it were in his power to control their fate. Near the end of *Mein Kampf*, after blaming the Jews for the defeat of Germany during World War I, Hitler suggests how he would have dealt with them: ''If at the beginning of the War and during the War twelve or fifteen thousand of these Hebrew corrupters of the people had been held under poison gas, as happened to hundreds of thousands of our very best German workers in the field, the sacrifice of millions at the front would not have been in vain.'' Now on the threshold of war, he made his intentions clear. On January 30, 1939, he addressed the Reichstag on the sixth anniversary of his seizure of power:

*And one more thing I would like now to state on this day memorable perhaps not only for us Germans. I have often been a prophet in my life and was gener-*

*ally laughed at. During my struggle for power, the Jews primarily received with laughter my prophecies that I would someday assume the leadership of the state and thereby of the entire Volk and then, among many other things, achieve a solution of the Jewish problem. I suppose that meanwhile the then resounding laughter of Jewry in Germany is now choking in their throats.*

*Today I will be a prophet again: If international finance Jewry within Europe and abroad should succeed once more in plunging the peoples into a world war, then the consequence will be not the Bolshevization of the world and therewith a victory of Jewry, but on the contrary, the destruction of the Jewish race in Europe.*

Once German troops entered Poland, they singled out the Jews for special treatment, moving them into ghettos and forcing them to wear yellow stars on their clothing. In Warsaw alone, hundreds of thousands of Jews were forced to exist in a cramped, bricked-in area, the Warsaw Ghetto. Until 1941, however, there was no systematic plan about what to do with the Jews. They were harassed, shot, there was even talk of deporting them all to the French island of Madagascar. But after the invasion of Russia, Hitler gave orders to find a more practical solution.

When talking about the extermination of the Jews, the Nazis always used innocuous, bland-sounding language. When they put thousands of people at a time into boxcars and sent them to death camps, they called the procedure "resettlement in the east." When the Nazis devised a comprehensive plan to destroy European Jewry they called it the "Final Solution."

To carry out their plans, the Nazis needed the cooperation of the country's Civil Service. Hitler, after all, wanted to kill eleven million Jews. It was a job neither the army nor the Nazi party could handle alone. His chief accomplices were Reinhard Heydrich and Heinrich Himmler. Heydrich presented the new plans to representatives of the state's bureaucracy at a conference in Berlin in January 1942. He was nervous about this meeting. He did not know how these legal experts and government bureaucrats would react to a large-scale, organized, and utterly merciless plan to murder men, women, and children. It would require the help of railway officials, architects, engineers, and even chemists to advise which poison was best to use on people. But no one objected.

A few days after this conference, Hitler told his friends over lunch that he wanted to be rid of all the Jews. ''One must act radically,'' he told them. ''When one pulls out a tooth, one does it with a single tug, and the pain quickly goes away. The Jew must clear out of Europe. . . . But if they refuse to go voluntarily I see no other solution but extermination.''

The Nazis employed two principal methods of murder. In Soviet territory, where partisan units and the Red Army were opposing them, the Nazis shot the Jews. Four special units, called *Einsatzgruppen*, special action groups, rounded up Jews and took them into secluded woods or ravines that offered convenient spots for mass graves. The victims often had to dig trenches, then strip before SS units shot them. Thousands could be killed in a single day. In Kiev and Kharkov, in Riga, Vilna, and Odessa once proud Jewish communities were decimated.


THE DEATH CAMPS

The Nazis, however, understood that such methods were not appropriate in Poland or Western Europe. The fighting was finished there. There were no battles to camouflage the work of organized murderers. Shooting was too expensive, too inefficient. It was bad for the morale of the soldiers who often got upset after killing helpless women and children. So the Final Solution took on a more calculating and efficient dimension. The Nazis decided to construct killing centers, concentration camps, whose principal function would be to murder people.

Trains brought Jews from Holland and France, from Germany, Czechoslovakia, and Austria to places called Auschwitz and Bergen-Belsen, Sobibor, and Treblinka. Locked into crowded boxcars, with hardly any food or water, they traveled for days or even weeks until reaching their destination. Many died on the trip from starvation and disease.

Once inside a camp like Auschwitz, the men and women were immediately separated. The great majority was then marched to gas chambers where hundreds of people at a time could be poisoned to death. The Nazis created an elaborate system to fool their victims. The paths were bordered with flowers. Sometimes a small orchestra played music as lines of people walked by. They were told there was work for them, that they needed different clothing. The guards gave them bars of soap as they walked into rooms outfitted with shower heads. What happened next was described by Rudolf Hess, the commandant of Auschwitz:

> The door would now be quickly screwed up and the gas discharged by the waiting disinfectors through vents in the ceilings of the gas chambers down a shaft that led to the floor. This insured the rapid distribution of the gas. It could be observed through the peephole in the door that those who were standing nearest to the induction vents were killed at once. It can be said that about one-third died straight away. The remainder staggered about and began to scream and struggle for air. The screaming, however, soon changed to the death rattle and in a few minutes all lay still.

Once the war began, the Jews had very little genuine opportunity to escape. By 1942 the trains to Auschwitz began delivering Jews from France, Belgium, Holland, and Croatia. The Jews of Norway arrived in November. In the spring of 1943 came Jews from Greece. Then the large ghettos of Poland, in Lodz and Bialystock, were liquidated. Jews from Minsk and Vilna soon followed. In October the Jews of southern France and Rome reached Auschwitz. In December the Jews of northern Italy arrived.

What happened in Hungary demonstrates the priority attached to the killing of Jews. Until 1944 Hungary provided a kind of haven for the Jews of Eastern Europe. About three hundred thousand managed to slip into Hungary to join an established community of a half million. Hungary had entered the war as an ally of Germany, hoping to gain territory in the east. It was not occupied by German troops. But all this changed in March 1944. With Soviet troops advancing, the Hungarian government began thinking of surrender. The Nazis then took the initiative, sending German soldiers into Hungary for the first time. Adolf Eichmann reached Budapest on March 19.

Eichmann's job was to arrange the deportation of Jews to the death camps in Poland. He had traveled across Europe throughout the war, arranging train schedules and bargaining with officials. He was an administrative genius. His career reached its culmination in Hungary. Within two months of his arrival trains to Auschwitz began departing from Budapest. At the same time, German forces were in a major military struggle, but Eichmann had full authority to order cattle cars and railroad lines for his purposes. In the middle of Germany's catastrophic retreat, Eichmann managed to send a half million Hungarian Jews by train to Auschwitz in less than two months. He could not have accomplished this extraordinary transfer of people without the approval of the highest authority in the Reich.

The Nazis took great pride in their campaign against the Jews. Heinrich Himmler directed the construction of the death camps. Speaking to a group of SS officers, he expressed his views on the Final Solution:

> *Most of you will know what it means when 100 corpses are lying side by side, when 500 are lying there or when 1000 are lying there. To have stuck this out and at the same time—apart from excep- tions due to human weaknesses—to have remained decent, that is what has made us hard.*

Eichmann, too, was not ashamed of his role in all this. At the Nuremberg trials for captured Nazi leaders, one of Eich- mann's colleagues reported that near the close of the war Eichmann said that "he would leap laughing into the grave because the feeling that he had 5 million people on his con- science would be for him a source of extraordinary satisfac- tion."

Unarmed and overwhelmed by brute force, most of the victims accepted death quietly, without resistance. There was no one to help them; no government tried to save them, to destroy the gas chambers or the railroad lines that carried them to their deaths. The Nazis also made it clear that death was not the worst possible fate. When prisoners resisted or tried to escape, they were often tortured or killed on the elec- trified barbed-wire fence that surrounded the camps and car- ried a current of six thousand volts.

## RESISTING THE OPPRESSOR

The Nazis, nonetheless, did meet opposition. Dutch workers went on strike to protest the deportation of their Jewish fel- low-citizens. The Germans declared martial law, arresting strike leaders and shooting members of the organized resistance movement. Still, it took four police battalions to crush the strike. Four hundred Jews were also picked up as hostages. The Nazis wanted to teach the Dutch a lesson. These four hundred went to Buchenwald, then to Mauthausen, a concentration camp in Austria, where they were all brutally tortured to death.

The most imaginative help came from the Danes. There was only a small Jewish community in Denmark, about eight thousand people. The Germans easily occupied the country in April 1940—there was no fighting. But on the day the country's Jews were required to wear a yellow star, the King of Denmark rode through the streets in an open, horse-drawn carriage, wearing a yellow star himself. The Germans waited until the fall of 1943 to round up the Jews of Denmark, but the government of Denmark knew of the plan and decided to protect them. Many were hidden from the Nazis in their neighbors' homes. The majority was secretly taken to Sweden by boat. When the Nazis came for the Jews, they found barely five hundred people, mostly elderly or sick people who had not learned how to escape.

The situation was much more desperate in Eastern Europe, but groups of Jews tried to resist as best they could. They escaped from ghettos in Lodz or Vilna, took refuge in the woods, and tried to obtain guns from other partisan resistance units. Five hundred Jews, for example, managed to get out of the Vilna ghetto. Their units—carrying names like "For Victory," "The Avengers," and "Death to Fascism"— fought the Nazis in surprise attacks.

A revolt even took place inside Treblinka. By the middle of 1943 nearly a million Jews had died in its gas chambers, but on August 2 six hundred prisoners armed with stolen guns and grenades attacked the Nazi guards, destroyed the gas chambers and the crematoria, and fled to the nearby Polish forests. Forty of them survived the war to bear witness.

The most famous and most desperate revolt took place

in Warsaw. By 1943 only a small percentage of Polish Jewry was still alive. Those remaining in the ghetto—over fifty thousand people, knew what had happened to their relatives, friends, and neighbors. They decided it was better to die fighting. The Jews had a handful of guns and a small supply of "molotov cocktails," bottles filled with gasoline and burning rags that explode on impact. The Germans were armed with airplanes, tanks, flame throwers, and howitzers. The height of the Warsaw Ghetto Uprising took place in April 1943. The Germans had to break into the ghetto, and the Jews made them fight for every building and city block.

One underground leaflet proudly explained their defiance:

> *Life belongs to us too! We too have a right to it! We only have to know how to fight for it! It is easy enough to live if they give you life as a gracious gift! It is not so easy when they want to snatch life away from you!*
>
> *Rise up, people, and fight for your lives!*
>
> *Every mother shall become a lioness defending her young! No longer shall a father quietly look upon the death of his children! The shame of the first act in our destruction shall not be repeated! May every house become a fortress! Rise up, people, and fight!!! Your salvation lies in fighting! He who fights for his life has the chance of saving himself! We rise up in the name of the fight for the lives of the helpless whom we wish to save and whom we must rouse to action!*

The report of the German commander, General Jurgen Stroop, confirmed the courage of the resisters:

> *Not infrequently, the Jews stayed in the burning buildings until, due to the heat and the fear of being*

*burned alive, they preferred to jump down from the upper stories, having first thrown down mattresses and other upholstery on the street. With their bones broken, they still tried to crawl across the street to blocks of buildings that were not yet, or only partially, on fire.*

It took the Germans a month to liquidate the remnants of the Warsaw Ghetto. But the Uprising haunted them for the rest of the war and became a symbol of defiance to Nazi brutality.

## DEFEAT ON THE EASTERN FRONT

In spite of Hitler's initial successes in the Soviet Union, he was not able to destroy the Red Army. Leningrad resisted capture. Moscow, too, held out, despite German advances into the city's suburbs. Hitler's plans were too ambitious. He dispersed his forces, thinking he could besiege Leningrad in the north, attack Moscow, and, at the same time, capture oil fields in the Caucasus. His generals advised him to concentrate German forces on Moscow, but Hitler dismissed their ideas, convinced the Red Army would collapse under all his pressure.

In addition, Hitler did not appreciate the importance of Russian weather conditions, especially in winter. He underestimated the transport problem, not taking into account the poor state of unpaved Russian roads whose dust and mud hurt the efficiency of his weapons. When his staff protested, suggesting the German armies slow their advance and fortify their positions, Hitler denounced them:

*Before I became Reich Chancellor, I used to think that the General Staff was like a mastiff which required a firm hand on its collar to prevent it from attacking everyone within reach. Since becoming Reich Chancellor I have realized that the German General Staff is not in the least like a mastiff. The General Staff has always sought to prevent me from doing what I considered necessary: The General Staff opposed rearmament, the occupation of the Rhineland, the invasion of Austria, the occupation of Czechoslovakia and, finally, even the war on Poland. . . . It is I who have always had to stir up this mastiff.*

Hitler contributed to his own defeat in another substantial way. Alfred Rosenberg, one of his oldest colleagues, understood that Stalin was hated by large portions of the Soviet population. Rosenberg wanted Germany to treat the Soviet people as anti-Stalinists rather than as enemies of Germany. That way they might greet the German armies as liberators. But Hitler rejected this advice. He personally ordered the shooting of all Soviet government and Communist Party officials. Any civilian caught with guns was also to be shot without trial. These brutal measures made it impossible for the Germans to gain the cooperation of the local inhabitants.

Hitler's luck ran out in January 1943. It had been his strategy to advance along a wide front in the east. But despite overwhelming odds, neither Leningrad nor Moscow surrendered to the Germans. Still Hitler pushed on, attempting also to capture Stalingrad, a large industrial city on the banks of the Volga. The German advance was halted here. The German Sixth Army, under General Friedrich Paulus, was about to be trapped by a superior Soviet force. General Paulus wanted to retreat, to consolidate his forces and save his army. But Hitler insisted that Paulus stand fast. He even listened to Göring who assured Hitler that the Luftwaffe could drop enough supplies to support the Sixth Army.

Hitler's optimism was unfounded and his mistakes contributed to the disastrous defeat. Paulus could not withstand the Russians and, under Hitler's orders, he was not permitted to retreat. By January 1943, after months of fighting, the defeat was total. Out of 265,000 men of the German Sixth Army, 100,000 were killed, 34,000 wounded, and 90,000 taken prisoner. From then on, Hitler could not stop the Soviet steamroller.

As the war dragged on and the scope of Germany's defeat became evident, Hitler grew increasingly isolated and hard to work with. For a great part of the war he lived below ground at his headquarters in East Prussia. By 1943 he no longer visited the front or toured factories. He learned of German defeats or temporary successes over the radio or telephone, never by direct observation.

His health was growing more precarious. He suffered from persistent insomnia which he would try to relieve by taking long walks at night in order to induce sleep. By 1943, although he was only fifty-four years old, he looked and felt like an old man. A slight curvature of the spine gave him a stooping posture. His left arm and leg exhibited nervous tremors. If he stood for too long, his knees would tremble. His doctors tried to treat him for fatigue, to get him to rest, but his principal doctor, Theo Morell, was incompetent. He gave Hitler too many drugs, especially for his frequent stomach pains and discomfort. These pills contained small quantities of strychnine and atropine, both poisons. The medication probably aggravated his condition. From the time of his mother's premature death, Hitler had always feared he would die before accomplishing his life work. By the middle of the war, he was obsessed with his health and the fear of death. He would complain about his stomach problems and frequently take his own pulse.

Hitler's health affected his judgment as a military and political leader. Before the war and during the initial years of military success, he was always ready to take a gamble, to challenge his opponents and, through bluff and surprise, gain the upper hand. But once his armies faced difficulties on the eastern front, Hitler did not have the patience to listen to the advice of his generals. He lost a necessary flexibility of mind which all commanders need when faced with different circumstances of position, men, and material in order to devise appropriate strategy. Hitler, for example, refused to allow his troops to evacuate conquered territory or to establish defensive positions behind his front lines. This policy was disastrous in the Soviet Union, especially when the Red Army went on the offensive. Hitler's troops had nothing to fall back on, making their retreat even more desperate. But Hitler persisted in his belief that the generals of World War I had had only one idea—to give ground—and he refused to repeat this mistake!

His stubbornness cost him dearly. He grew suspicious of any criticism or ideas that differed from his own. Most of his senior officers resigned or were dismissed, including many generals and field marshals whose experience and military training would have made them valuable advisers.

## THE UNITED STATES
## ENTERS THE WAR

In the west, as well as on the eastern front, Hitler faced impending disaster  England had remained free and after the attack on Pearl Harbor on December 7, 1941, America's entry into the war assured the Allies' ultimate victory. Hitler, at first, was heartened by the news from Pearl Harbor—the Japanese attack on America's naval base in Hawaii. He respected the Japanese. "We cannot lose the war!" he proclaimed to an aide. "Now we have a partner who has not been defeated in three thousand years." Four days after Pearl Harbor, Hitler declared war on the United States. He was under an obligation by treaty with the Japanese to fight alongside them. Speaking to the Reichstag, Hitler denounced President Roosevelt. "First he incites war, then falsifies the causes, then odiously wraps himself in a cloak of Christian hypocrisy and slowly but surely leads mankind to war."

In spite of the Japanese attack, President Roosevelt regarded Germany as the greater enemy. He wanted to defeat Hitler first, then deal with Japan. For this reason American troops joined the war in North Africa and in the Mediterranean Sea. But it was not until June 6, 1944, that the Allies were ready to open the long-awaited second front: the invasion of Europe across the English Channel.

The Allies succeeded in fooling the Germans. Reports reached Berlin of major landings near Normandy, but General Alfred Jodl, head of Hitler's army planning staff, thought they were a diversionary tactic. It was three in the morning, and he refused to wake Hitler with the news. Hitler learned of the invasion at nine o'clock. He too believed the main attack would come at Calais, where the Channel is its narrowest. (This had been his proposed strategy four years earlier when he considered invading England.) The Allies, however, concentrated their forces at Normandy, farther south.

Even when it became evident that the invasion was taking place in Normandy, there would have still been time to throw back the Allies. The Allied bridgehead was vulnerable to counterattack. But Hitler refused to give his field commanders responsibility to act as they saw fit. Within a week the Germans were forced to retreat. On June 17 Hitler drove to the front. "He looked pale and sleepless," recalled General Hans Speidel, "playing nervously with his glasses and an array of colored pencils which he held between his fingers." Later, at lunch, two of his bodyguards tasted his food before he would eat. Hitler, apparently, distrusted his own military officers; within a month, he would have ample proof of their loss of faith in him.

## THE JULY CONSPIRACY

Since Hitler had reached power in 1933, there had been several unsuccessful attempts to assassinate him. Before the war began, a number of army officers hoped to arrest him; they were opposed to his war plans and foresaw only disaster for Germany. But nothing came of their plans. By 1944, though, it was clear the war was lost. The Allies had successfully invaded Europe, while in the east Soviet troops were punishing German armies. Yet Hitler insisted on fighting. He would not consider surrender or negotiating an armistice. He understood that his own life would end when the war was over, so he prolonged the fighting, sending German troops to needless death and subjecting German cities to Allied bombing. Roosevelt, Churchill, and Stalin demanded unconditional surrender. But Hitler refused to give in. Only his death could end the fighting.

By July 1944 a large conspiracy, involving high-ranking officers and government officials, planned to assassinate Hitler, then accomplish a military takeover in Berlin, Paris, and Vienna. The plan was led by Count Klaus von Stauffenberg, a lieutenant colonel who had been severely injured in the war when his car ran over a mine. He had lost an eye, his right hand, and two fingers of the left hand. But Stauffenberg recovered and dedicated his life to killing Hitler. Stauffenberg and his fellow conspirators hoped to take over the government and open negotiations with the western allies. They did not want to see Germany destroyed or allow the Red Army to advance and occupy further territory.

On July 20, 1944, Stauffenberg visited Wolf's Lair, one of Hitler's secret headquarters in East Prussia, to attend a staff meeting. In his briefcase he carried a bomb designed to end

Hitler's life. While Hitler was going over some maps on a large table, Stauffenberg placed the briefcase where Hitler usually stood, but by a quirk of fate someone moved the briefcase a few feet, to the other side of a thick, wooden table support. When the bomb exploded, Hitler was injured, but he was not killed. His skin was riddled with splinters of wood; more than a hundred were removed from his legs alone. His face was slightly cut and his forehead bruised. His right hand was sprained and the hair on the back of his head was singed by the heat of the explosion. His hearing was impaired, especially in his left ear, and his sense of balance was affected. He complained of even worse insomnia than he had experienced before.

If the plot had succeeded, the war might have ended sooner and countless lives would have been saved. Instead Hitler regarded his survival as a divine gesture, a sign that God wanted him to complete his mission and lead Germany to victory. Count von Stauffenberg and several hundred others were arrested and executed. Hitler took his revenge. But his dream of victory was a delusion. By July 1944 the German armies could not hold out much longer.

## THE FINAL DAYS

Faced with defeat on all fronts, Hitler was barely capable of guiding his armies. One of his doctors, Erwin Giesing, was shocked by his appearance. "Hitler gave the impression of being prematurely aged . . . worn out and exhausted, a man who had to husband his strength. . . . His shoulders sagged, his chest was hollow and his breathing superficial." He kept insisting that his luck would change, that a new weapon—the V-1 and V-2 rockets, perhaps, or a new type of airplane—would save Germany. He also believed that the alliance of America, England, and Russia could not last, that the western allies would understand that only a strong Ger-

many could hold back Stalin. But his luck did not improve. His determination to keep fighting made him personally responsible for the colossal destruction and loss of life that Germany suffered in the closing year of the war. This was why Count von Stauffenberg had wanted to kill him.

Hitler spent the last four months of the war in an underground fortified bunker beneath the Reich Chancellery building in Berlin. He was totally isolated, accompanied only by his secretaries, the faithful Eva Braun, his quack doctor Theo Morell, and a few, still-loyal generals.

Adolf Hitler could not face the challenge of defeat. He could not accept his own responsibility for German reverses. After surviving von Stauffenberg's bomb, Hitler declared: "I am beginning to doubt whether the German people is worthy of my great ideals." A month later he told a group of Nazi party leaders that "If the German people was to be conquered in the struggle then it had been too weak to face the test of history, and was fit only for destruction." Hitler claimed that he wanted to save Germany, but he was perfectly willing to sacrifice Germany, to see the entire country destroyed if his own dream were not fulfilled. As early as 1934 he had warned that "Even if we could not conquer, we should drag half the world into destruction with us, and leave no one to triumph over Germany. There will not be another 1918. We shall not surrender."

*This photograph of Hitler with Eva Braun was made at his retreat, Berchtesgaden, toward the end of the war, before they moved into the underground bunker in Berlin.*

With defeat imminent, Hitler declared a policy of "World Power or Ruin." Confined to his bunker in Berlin, he issued orders for the blowing up of German towns and factories, dams and bridges. He wanted farms burned and livestock killed. Had Hitler's instructions been fully carried out, the German people would have faced widespread famine.

Albert Speer, one of Hitler's most loyal colleagues, worked hard to oppose this plan. Speer was a talented architect and a brilliant organizer who had devised enormous rallies to celebrate Nazism in the 1930s. During the war he was given control of all armament production, plus the building and maintenance of communications and the direction of German industry. Speer was a uniquely gifted man among Hitler's corrupt and cynical associates. He, too, believed in Hitler, but he did not relinquish all his ability to think for himself. For ten years he had remained near the center of political power. His efforts during the war to maintain production despite Allied bombing were so successful that historians believe he may have prolonged the fighting for two years. But only when Hitler proposed to destroy all that Speer had constructed did Speer decide to oppose him. So Speer issued orders of his own, hoping to save the remnants of German civilization and industry for those who survived the war.

Hitler learned of Speer's activity and summoned him to the bunker. His statement to Speer expressed his own hatred for the German people:

*If the war is to be lost, the nation also will perish. This fate is inevitable. There is no need to consider the basis even of a most primitive existence any longer. On the contrary it is better to destroy even that, and to destroy it ourselves. The nation has proved itself weak, and the future belongs solely to the stronger Eastern nation [the Soviet Union]. Besides, those who*

*remain after the battle are of little value; for the good
have fallen.*

At the end Hitler could not grasp what was really happening.
He still spoke of victory. He would not tolerate talk of defeat.
In spite of his physical deterioration, his personal charisma
and authority were intact. In March, a month before Hitler's
death, Field Marshal Ernst Busch came directly to the bunker
from the front, still wearing his battle-stained uniform. He
understood that Germany was collapsing. He wanted to convince Hitler to give in. But instead Hitler was able to convince
him that final victory was still possible, although his arguments
were nothing more than wishful thinking.

As Soviet tanks closed in, Hitler ordered counterattacks
by troops that did not exist, led by commanders with no
equipment or means to rally their men. Only a few dozen followers stayed with Hitler in the bunker. They could hear the
bombardment outside and received reports of Berlin neighborhoods falling to Soviet troops.

Hitler did not want to be captured. He made plans for his
own suicide. But first, in the early morning hours of April 29,
1945, he married his longtime companion, Eva Braun. Hitler
had never considered marriage before. He thought it would
interfere with his work and, perhaps, make him seem too
human when he preferred to be regarded as a messiah. But
now he wanted to repay Eva Braun for her years of loyalty to
him by formalizing their relationship. So they were married in a
ceremony witnessed by eight of Hitler's associates.

Outside the bunker, Berlin was falling rapidly. Soviet
troops were seen in a street nearby. Hitler could not face the
end. On the afternoon of April 30 he and Eva Braun retired to
their suite. They sat down on a couch. Eva took poison and
died instantly. Hitler shot himself in the right temple with a
pistol. Their bodies were dragged outside and burned.

This was not the final terrible event to occur in the bunker. Joseph Goebbels, his wife Magda, and their six young children were in the bunker as well. Rather than face capture, he too decided to kill himself. While their children were sleeping, Magda slipped poison into their mouths. Then Goebbels and his wife went outside the bunker where a German soldier shot them dead. Their bodies, like Hitler's were also burned.

The war was over in Europe. Hitler's one-thousand-year Reich came to an end after twelve years, three months, and eight days.

# THE AFTERMATH

# 5

To evaluate the historical impact of Adolf Hitler, it is necessary to acknowledge at the outset a fundamental problem in
seeking to understand him at all. Adolf Hitler, by any conventional standard of human psychology, was a lunatic. He had
colossal delusions of grandeur, believing that his own obses-
sions, fears, and dreams about German history and Jews, for
example, should become the absolute objectives of an entire
nation. He could not permit any other value—human life,
compassion, the sovereignty of other countries—to interfere
with his dreams.

When he addressed crowds, he used the most extravagant style of vocabulary and diction, shaking his fists, shouting, exhausting himself for hours in front of an audience. It is
difficult for people today to understand the effect of these
speeches, yet Hitler provoked intense loyalty and fanatical
trust from his listeners. Albert Speer recognized this power:

*Hitler was one of those inexplicable historical phe-
nomena which emerge at rare intervals among man-*

*kind. His person determined the fate of the nation. He alone placed it, and kept it, upon the path which has led it to this dreadful ending. The nation was spellbound by him as a people has rarely been in the whole of history.*

Even in the final stages of the war—when German defeat was certain, when her cities were continually attacked by enemy bombers, when food was rationed, when there was not enough coal to heat German homes, in short when the extent of the disaster Hitler had brought was clear to any objective observer—he still had the loyalty and faith of a majority of the population.

Something in his personality, his failings as well as his abilities, corresponded to a need in the German people. The humiliation of defeat in World War I, the economic troubles of the 1920s, the lack of democratic traditions, the cultural longing for order and stability, the distrust of foreigners and Jews—all contributed to the outbreak of hatred that engulfed Germany.

Adolf Hitler was at the center of this upheaval and it is hard to imagine the extravagant crimes of Nazism or the extravagant dimensions of the war without him. Hitler believed in himself and his messianic mission. Writing in Landsberg prison in 1924, he said about himself:

*At long intervals in human history, it may occasionally happen that the practical politician and the political philosopher are one. The more intimate the union, the greater his political difficulties. Such a man does not labor to satisfy the demands that are obvious to every philistine; he reaches out towards ends that are comprehensible only to the few. Therefore his life is torn between hatred and love. The protest of the present generation, which does not understand him, wrestles with the recognition of posterity, for whom he also works.*

This absolute confidence made Hitler's appeal irresistible.

But what did Hitler want? His career began in the years following World War I when Germany was forced to accept the Versailles Treaty. Hitler had served in the trenches. He took Germany's defeat as a personal insult—as did many veterans—and he vowed to reverse the war's outcome. This was a formative experience for him and explains why he declared during the Second World War that Germany would not surrender, that there would not be another 1918.

But as we have seen, Hitler's ambitions went far beyond what might be considered the legitimate or at least the natural and altogether expected wishes of a resurgent German nationalism. He had radical ideas. He wanted not only to restore Germany as the dominant power in Europe but also to destroy European civilization and create a Nazi empire in the center of Europe. To accomplish this he wanted to consolidate Europe's German-speaking population into one large nation, incorporating Austria and parts of Czechoslovakia and France into a greater Reich. He then wanted to expand this Reich to the east, taking land from Poland and the Soviet Union, giving Germany what he called "living space." In order to do this, he intended to kill millions of Poles and Russians. Finally, Hitler wanted to murder all the Jews of Europe. His other goals, including victory in the war, were of less importance to him than this most terrible idea.

Only a madman could have dreamed these dreams. Only a political genius could have mobilized public support for them. Only an original military thinker could have come as close as he did to making them all come true. In the end, however, Hitler was defeated, and the political and geographic changes in Europe which his war produced were the opposite of what he intended.

On the eve of World War II Hitler's ideological enemy, the

Soviet Union, was a militarily weak country. Over the winter of 1939, during its short-lived war with Finland, the Red Army proved to be ill-equipped for modern warfare. Yet by 1945 the Soviet Union was in control of Eastern Europe and occupied a large portion of Germany itself. Today, decades later, the Soviet Union still maintains political and military control of most of Eastern Europe. Its territory also expanded, with the forced inclusion of the Baltic States—Lithuania, Latvia, and Estonia—and changes in its borders with Poland and Romania. It was Hitler who gave Stalin the opportunity to expand his empire.

The United States, too, was not a major military power until World War II. In the preceding decade, the 1930s, the United States had suffered a severe economic upheaval—the Great Depression. But the Japanese attack on Pearl Harbor on December 7, 1941, and Germany's declaration of war brought the United States into the conflict. Within a short time the nation's industrial capacity turned to wartime production. By the end of the war the United States and the Soviet Union were dominant world superpowers, an outcome Hitler did not foresee but which his actions made possible.

As for Western Europe, Great Britain emerged a victor in the war, but the war began the breakup of the British Empire. France was defeated and Germany itself was left in ruins, occupied by foreign armies and finally divided into separate countries. This division embodies to this day the terrible price the German people had to pay for the policies of Adolf Hitler.

Even the destruction of the Jews, which Hitler regarded as his greatest achievement, had an unforeseen and unintended consequence: the establishment of the first sovereign independent Jewish state in two thousand years. After the war the international community felt a sense of guilt for the suffering of the Jewish people. In 1947 the General Assembly of the United Nations voted to partition the territory of Palestine into Arab and Jewish areas. On May 14, 1948, the Jews, led by David Ben-Gurion, declared the establishment of Israel.

These political and geographic changes were not the only consequences of Hitler's program. His conduct of the war affected the morality of his allies as well as his enemies. In 1937 German and Italian aircraft leveled the town of Guérnica in the Spanish Civil War. This was a military experiment, the first mass bombing of a city. By the early months of World War II attacks on unarmed civilians and urban populations were commonplace. In Warsaw and Rotterdam, London and Coventry, throughout occupied territory in Russia, the Germans deliberately destroyed nonmilitary objectives. After Reinhard Heydrich was killed by Czech underground fighters in 1942, the Nazis murdered *all* the male inhabitants of the Czech village of Lidice. More than thirteen hundred Czechs were killed in revenge for Heydrich's assassination.

The Allies responded with cruelty of their own. On February 13, 1945, British and American bombers destroyed the old city of Dresden. It had no strategic value, no military importance. Yet the Allies attacked it, killing tens of thousands of civilians.

Hitler's early victories compelled the west to seek new and more effective weapons in order to stop him. One of these weapons was the atom bomb. The United States originally thought it would need the atom bomb to defeat Germany. Instead two bombs were dropped on Japan in August 1945. There were serious military reasons for destroying Hiroshima and Nagasaki with atomic weapons. The United States had already destroyed Tokyo through aerial bombing, killing about a hundred thousand civilians, but the Japanese still refused to surrender. They were preparing to defend their home islands with all the men and material they could muster. An American invasion of Japan could have caused a million U.S. casualties alone and prolonged the war another year at

*May, 1945: American soldiers in Cologne, Germany,
march past a woman who views with dismay the rubble
that was once a busy shopping district.*

least. At the same time, one cannot help but wonder if such weapons of destruction would ever have been employed if Hitler had not already raised the acceptable level of brutality during wartime.

The rule of Adolf Hitler was a disaster for Germany. When he came to power in 1933 Germany, with all its economic and social problems, was still a wealthy country. Its industry was the most advanced in Europe. Its social services were the most modern on the continent. Its universities were distinguished, its newspapers free, intelligent, and well-informed. Today, Germany is a divided country.

The Federal Republic of Germany is a prosperous industrial democracy, allied with the United States. In some respects, it has tried to confront the traumatic experience of Hitler's rule. Financial reparations were paid to Jewish survivors and others who lost relatives and property because of persecution. Former Nazi officials have been exposed and brought to trial for their participation in Hitler's crimes. But today, nearly four decades since the close of the war, West Germany still carries the burden of guilt and memory.

The German Democratic Republic—East Germany—is also a legacy of Hitler's defeat. Occupied by Soviet troops since 1945, East Germany is a strong industrial power. But it is not a democracy. Its citizens are not permitted free and easy contact with family members in West Germany. Literature is heavily censored. Artistic expression is severely controlled. Independent political activity is forbidden. The citizens of East Germany survived the war only to be overwhelmed by communist domination.

None of this could have happened without the rise and defeat of Adolf Hitler.

# FOR
# FURTHER
# READING

Dolan, Edward F. *Adolf Hitler: A Portrait in Tyranny*. New York: Dodd, Mead, 1981. (A comprehensive, highly readable biography of Hitler for young adults.)

Forman, James. *Ceremonies of Innocence*. New York: Hawthorn, 1970. (This novel describes the ill-fated group of young Germans known as the White Rose Resistance who opposed Hitler and were caught and executed during the war.)

Forman, James D. *Nazism*. New York: Franklin Watts, 1978. (A history of Hitler's rise to power that emphasizes the development of Nazi ideology and its practice in German foreign and domestic policies.)

Forman, James. *The Survivor*. New York: Farrar, Straus & Giroux, 1976. (A Jewish teenager from Holland is arrested with his family and deported to Auschwitz. The boy alone survives and returns to his hometown at the close of the war.)

Koehn, Ilse. *Mischling, Second Degree*. New York: Greenwillow, 1977. (An autobiographical novel of a young German girl with one Jewish grandparent. After the Nuremburg laws are put into effect, her life changes.)

Meltzer, Milton. *Never to Forget*. New York: Dell, 1976. (A general history of the Holocaust.)

Orgel, Doris. *The Devil in Vienna*. New York: Dial, 1978. (A novel about two girls in Vienna—one a Christian, the other a Jew—and what happens to their friendship when Hitler takes over Austria.)

Richter, Hans. *Friedrich*. New York: Holt, Rinehart & Winston, 1970. (An autobiographical novel about a Jewish boy and his German friend in West Germany.)

Samuels, Gertrude. *Mottele*. New York: Harper & Row, 1976. (A fictionalized account of a true story about a twelve-year-old boy who joins a group of Jewish partisan fighters.)

Suhl, Yuri. *On the Other Side of the Gate*. New York: Franklin Watts, 1975. (This novel concerns a young couple who decide to have a child after the Nazis have forbidden the Jews to bear children.)

von Staden, Wendelgard. *Darkness Over the Valley: Growing Up in Nazi Germany*. New Haven, Conn.: Ticknor & Fields, 1981. (The author, a niece of Hitler's first foreign minister, grew up on a large estate near a concentration camp. Her book tells how she and her family tried to help the prisoners.)

Wiesel, Elie. *Night*. New York: Bantam, 1982. (A short, eloquent novel about the author's deportation to Auschwitz and the death of his father.)

Teachers and students might also be interested in a new curriculum on the Holocaust and the Armenian Genocide devised in Brookline, Massachusetts:

Strom, Margot Stern and William S. Parsons. *Facing History and Ourselves: The Holocaust and Human Behavior*. Brookline, Mass.: Intentional Educations, 1982.

# INDEX

in World War I, 16, 17, 19; in
World War II, 77, 78, 79, 80, 98
Free Corps, 24, 25

German National Party, 58
German Workers' Party, 26–29
Germany: and *Anschluss*, 66–69;
as "Aryan race," 36–37;
Czechoslovakia invaded by, 69–
72; defeated in Soviet Union,
93–95, 96, 98; depression in,
45, 47; East vs. West, 113; Hitler as Chancellor of, 48, 51;
1920s inflation, 31, 38; 1930s
growth, 51–72; Poland invaded
by, 72, *76*, 77; post-World War I
socialism in, 20, 25, 26–27;
post-World War II, 107–113; rearmament of, 61–65; Soviet
Union invaded by, 81-82; as Soviet World War II ally, 72, 79,
80; and Versailles Treaty, 23–
24, 25, 61, 62, 64; as Weimar
Republic, 25–28; in World War I,
16–20; in World War II, 75–104.
*See also* Nazi Party; Hitler; Third
Reich
Goebbels, Joseph, 42, 47, 51, 53,
104
Göring, Hermann, 43, 51, 55, 56,
59, 60, 78, 94

Himmler, Heinrich, 59, *63*, 87, 90
Hiroshima, 111
Hitler, Adolf, *18*, *39*, *46*, *57*, *63*,
*76*, *100*; artistic pursuits of, 8–
16; assassination attempts on,
98–99; birth of, 5; as Chancellor
of Germany, 48, 51; childhood
of, 5–9; defeat of, 99–104; early
anti-Semitism of, 14, 28–29, 30,
36–37, 40, 44, 82, 84, 109; and
Eva Braun, 43, 44, 69, *100*,
101, 103; and German Workers'

party, 26–29; and growth of
Nazi Party, 29–48; health of, 95,
96, 99, 107; imprisonment of,
35–38; insanity of, 107; Jews
persecuted by, in World War II,
82, 87–90, 91; marriage of, 44,
103; *Mein Kampf* by, 8, 15, 16,
26, 36–37, 62, 86; in Munich,
15–16, 30–34, 40, 41; and
1930s Third Reich, 51–72; post-
war consequences of, 110–113;
suicide of, 1, 44, 103; and Weimar Republic, 25–58; and World
War I, 16–20, 108, 109; and
World War II, 75–104
Holland, 79, 89
Hungary, Jews in, 89

Israel, 84, 110–111
Italy, 65, 66

Japan, 72, 110; in World War II,
75, 96–97
Jews: Austrian, 68, 88; in concentration camps, 87–90, 91; and
Crystal Night, 84–85; Danish,
91; and early Hitler anti-Semitism, 14, 38–39, 40, 41, 36–37,
38, 40, 44, 68, 82, 84–86, 109;
and "Final Solution," 86–90;
Hungarian, 90; Israel established
by, 110–111; Nuremberg Laws
against, 84; Polish, 82, 86, 89,
91–93; revolts of, 90–93; Soviet,
82, 87; World War II Nazi persecution of, 82, 87–90, 91. *See
also* Anti-Semitism

Luftwaffe, 78, 80

Marx, Karl, 15, 16, 19
Marxism, 15–16, 40
*Mein Kampf* (Hitler), 8, 15, 16, 26,
36–37, 62, 86